Abducted

Abducted

HOW PEOPLE COME TO BELIEVE
THEY WERE KIDNAPPED BY ALIENS

SUSAN A. CLANCY

HARVARD UNIVERSITY PRESS
Cambridge, Massachusetts
London, England
2005

Library of Congress Cataloging-in-Publication Data

Clancy, Susan A.
  Abducted : how people come to believe they were kidnapped
by aliens / Susan A. Clancy
    p. cm.
  Includes bibliographical references (p.) and index.
  ISBN 0-674-01879-6 (alk. paper)
  1. Alien abduction. I. Title.

BF2050.C56 2005
001.942—dc22   2005050245

To my husband,
Niels Ketelhohn
(the alien who abducted me),
and our two daughters,
Caroline and Elinor

Acknowledgments

This book could not have been written without Rich McNally and Elizabeth Knoll. I thank Rich for his teaching, guidance, and advice over the past ten years. Had it not been for him, I'd probably still be struggling to attach electrodes to drunk lab subjects in William James Hall. His hard work, prolific writing, and scientific clearheadedness are an inspiration to his students and colleagues.

Before I met Elizabeth, my discussions of my research were primarily confined to cocktail party conversation. Not only did she see the potential for a book, but she encouraged me to write it, guiding me step by step through the process and helping to shape the book into something I can be proud of.

Thanks also to Maria Ascher for her thorough and inspired editing of the text (she managed to maintain my voice while clearing up syntactic oddities and grammatical errors); to Harvard University and INCAE in Central America for their institutional support during the writing process; to the abductees who generously shared their experiences with me (needless to say, all of their names have been changed); and to my friends and family for all their love, enthusiasm, and support.

Contents

Abducted

Introduction

Will Andrews is an articulate, handsome forty-two-year-old. He's a successful chiropractor, lives in a wealthy American suburb, and has a strikingly attractive wife and twin boys, age eight. The only glitch in this picture of domestic bliss is that his children are not his wife's—they are the product of an earlier infidelity. To complicate matters further, the biological mother is an extraterrestrial.

In Will's mind, alien abductions are real. For the past ten years he has had vivid memories of having been repeatedly taken away by "beings" and medically, psychologically, and sexually experimented on. During his abductions, he became close to his "alien guide"—a streamlined, sylph-like creature. Although they didn't communicate verbally, he feels they became "spiritually connected" and their connection resulted in a number of hybrid babies. He never sees his children, but he feels their presence. "I know they're out there, and they know who I am."

Despite the fact that his abductions were traumatic—terrifying and often painful—he is happy he was "chosen." Because of them, his life has changed. "I was dispirited, confused, going through a down-cycle in my life and a bad patch in my relationship. . . . I was ready to just give up. I didn't know what was wrong, but I knew something was missing. Today, things are different. I feel great. I know there's something out there—much bigger, more important than we are—and for some reason they chose to make their presence known to me. I have a connection with them. What I do in this life has become less important to me—the meaning of today, of now. The beings are learning from us and us from them, and ultimately a new world is being created. And I'll have a part in it, either directly or through the twins."

While Will's life improved, his wife found herself confused, angry, and alienated. "This was my husband and all of a sudden he goes from being a normal guy, maybe a little depressed, to being . . . well . . . kind of nutty, I guess. I don't believe him, but I don't disbelieve him either. I really don't think he's making this up. I think something *did* happen to him that's been life-changing. I just don't know what it was. I really wish it didn't involve . . . well . . . the sex part, the spiritual connection he talks about. In some ways, I feel that what happened to him must have to do with our relationship. Something must have been missing, and I feel . . . a bit angry and sad. Would things have been different if we'd been able to have kids? Then again, it all seems so crazy that I don't know what to believe. . . . But I can tell you we're pretty happy now. . . . Things are better. . . . Basically I deal with it by trying not to think about it too much."

*   *   *

In the past three decades, claims of abduction by space aliens have become increasingly common. Beginning with Betty and Barney Hill's widely reported claims in the 1960s, sensationalized by Whitley Strieber's bestselling books in the 1980s, and ratified by Harvard Medical School's John Mack in the 1990s, the notion of alien abductions has become well known. There are probably few people in America between the ages of ten and sixty who are unfamiliar with the popular image of the alien or the basic plot of the standard alien-abduction story.[1]

Americans not only are familiar with the idea of abductions, but apparently are starting to believe in them. Polls suggest that about 93 percent of the population believe that extraterrestrials exist, and 27 percent believe that the earth has been visited by aliens. The belief in aliens has increased significantly in the past two decades (along with belief in spiritual healing, extrasensory perception, and communication with the dead). Approximately 85 percent of adults believe there is good evidence that life exists on other planets, and approximately half of those think it is possible that aliens have abducted humans.[2] One CNN/Time poll showed that 80 percent of Americans believe that the U.S. government is hiding knowledge of the existence of extraterrestrial life forms.[3] For what it's worth, in the past three years I've asked just about all the people I know whether they believe that extraterrestrial life exists. No one has given me a flat no. "The universe is huge. Why would we be alone?"

Still, claims of alien abduction have not been taken seriously by most members of the scientific community.[4] From their perspective, there are no compelling data that aliens even exist, never mind that people are being abducted, so why bother to investigate? Since anecdotal reports, no matter how compelling and impassioned, do not count as scientific evidence, and since other types of data are so thin as to be translucent, research on this topic has been primarily confined to enthusiastic fringe groups with no formal scientific training (for example, the Mutual UFO Network, Inc., commonly known as MUFON) and a few scattered academics who aren't afraid to sacrifice their professional reputations.

One of these academics was John Mack, a psychiatrist on the faculty of Harvard Medical School for almost fifty years and the founder of the Department of Psychiatry at Cambridge Hospital, in Cambridge, Massachusetts. Until the mid-1990s he was best known for his Pulitzer Prize–winning biography of Lawrence of Arabia.[5] Today he is known for another book entirely, one whose title needs no explaining—*Abduction: Human Encounters with Aliens.*

In the 1980s Mack became so interested in claims of alien abduction that he began using hypnosis to retrieve alien-abduction memories from interested participants, memories that he believed were real. In 1994, the year *Abduction* came out, he stated: "There is no evidence that anything other than what abductees are telling us has happened to them. . . . The people with whom I have been working are telling the truth." After his book received international attention and flabbergasted his colleagues, Harvard Medical School formed an ad hoc committee to investigate his work with abductees. The goal of the investigation, which took fifteen months, was not to challenge Mack's right to choose his research topics, but to ensure that whatever topic he chose was studied in a scholarly fashion. This was problematic for Mack because even he thought it was impossible to study the issue of alien abductions in a scientific manner. "It just doesn't fit into the Western rationalist tradition of science."[6]

I met John Mack only once. It was in 1999, at a publicity event for his book *Passport to the Cosmos*.[7] We spoke briefly. He was surrounded by a cluster of young women, groupie-like in their admiration for him and their desire for his attention. At seventy-three, he had good bone structure beneath his deeply lined skin; his eyes were a compelling steely blue; he carried himself regally. Though he wasn't much interested in talking to me, he was polite and suggested we meet for lunch.

Lunch never happened and it never will. In September 2004, as this book was in the final stages of preparation, John Mack was hit by a bus in London. According to the press, he died instantly. I was devastated. It had been my fondest hope that he would write a review of *Abducted*. I'd heard he was working on another book, examining the clash between scientific materialism and a nonrational point of view. In a *Psychology Today* article in 2003, Mack had been quoted as saying that when it came to studying the alien-abduction phenomenon, he and skeptical investigators like me were "in different firmaments."[8] Perhaps our two books might have fostered understanding between us.

The cold shoulder this topic has received from more conventional scientists is unfortunate, not because aliens are abducting earthlings—all the available evidence indicates they're not—but because so many people seem to *believe* they are. Why is this? It's definitely not because the abductees are crazy. Data from multiple studies indicate that abductees are no more likely than anyone else to suffer from psychiatric disorders. They may score high on measures of creativity, or proneness to fantasy, or intense visual imagery, but so do a lot of people who have never claimed contact with aliens.[9]

Why all this interest in alien abductions? Some researchers attribute it to the media's frequent references to extraterrestrials. Studies indicate that simply reading about an abduction claim in the newspaper can increase an individual's belief in the phenomenon.[10] Interesting as such findings are, however, the prevalence of media coverage does not explain just why so many people come to believe that *they themselves* have been abducted. Who are these individuals, and what are they like? What are the experiences they report? How do their beliefs develop, and what purposes do they serve? These, I believe, are interesting and important questions, and the purpose of this book is to offer the beginnings of an answer.

For many scientists, it is much easier to conclude that the question has already been answered—that such believers are scientifically illiterate, cognitively challenged, logically impaired, or (as one Nobel Prize winner succinctly phrased it) "talking complete and utter nonsense."[11]

But while there can be no doubt that some people *do* have trouble thinking scientifically, and that all of us have a tendency to adopt and endorse attractive ideas and beliefs without solid evidence, this "thinking gone wrong" hypothesis doesn't help. It's too broad. It might explain why people believe weird things, but not why they believe in one specific weird thing—namely, that they were abducted by space aliens. Problems with clear thinking are ubiquitous. All humans, including scientists, are occasionally guilty of credulity and insufficient skepticism.

If we really want to understand and learn from alien-abduction claims, we need to do more than dismiss them as ignorance. Though it's easy (and sometimes fun) to laugh, once the laughter dies we realize we have achieved nothing. In order to understand the origin and appeal of such bizarre beliefs, we need to know something about the individuals who hold them. How do they think? How do they remember? What sort of people are they? Many behavioral, social, and cognitive scientists have conducted studies useful to an investigation of this topic. Memory researchers have taught us about the nature of false memories; sleep researchers illuminate the perplexing phenomenon of sleep paralysis; and psychophysiologists have been teasing out the relationship between belief and emotion. Sociologists and anthropologists have examined the sociocultural roots of the typical alienabduction narrative; and clinical psychologists and psychiatrists have studied the personality characteristics of individuals with alien-abduction beliefs.

But although a synthesis of this research could go a long way toward explaining those beliefs, it would be far from convincing to the actual believers. The truth is that most alien abductees *are* aware of the sleep paralysis hypothesis, and the role that hypnosis plays in false-memory creation, and the widespread cultural availability of the alien-abduction script. They just don't care. To them, such findings are unappealing—indeed, stunningly unpersuasive. After all, they're the ones who were abducted—the ones who experienced the fear and horror. And when you pit the cold, remote virtues of scientific data against the immediacy of personal experience, science is bound to lose. You simply cannot tell abductees that their memories have resulted from a toxic combination of memory distortion, hypnosis, and watching too many *X-Files* episodes. You'll encounter only denial, anger, blank stares, or condescending smiles.

Abductees do not believe what they believe because of scientific evidence. Even John Mack admitted that belief in alien abductions is independent of any objective data. The only way to understand "why people believe weird things" (as skeptic Michael Shermer puts it) is to *ask them*. Over the past five years, I have talked with hundreds of believers—ranging from hardcore abductees with hybrid babies to those who simply saw strange lights in the sky and wondered about them—as well as with family members, colleagues, and people sitting next to me on the train. Why don't believers think sleep paralysis is relevant to explaining abduction experiences? Why do they think that some people get "chosen" and others don't? Why do they continue to undergo hypnosis, even though they know it may cause memory distortion? Why, in the absence of any scientific data, do they believe aliens exist?

What has emerged is that most people who find alien-abduction experiences compelling do so for three main reasons. First, the abduction memories and the concomitant emotions *feel* real to them. Second, they find the similarities among individual abduction accounts—the consistency among the stories—very persuasive. And third, they're struck by the sheer number and variety of people who believe the same things.

Over and over again I've been asked: It if didn't happen, then why do I have these horrible memories? If it didn't happen, then why do we all tell the same stories? If it didn't happen, then why do so many different kinds of people believe it? These are excellent questions, and almost everybody asks them—not just the staunch believer but any inquisitive person who hears about the abduction experience. They are what *most* people find compelling or confusing about the alien-abduction experience. And best of all, I think they are eminently answerable.

I'd like to illuminate the alien-abduction phenomenon by tackling it from the perspective of the believers themselves. One scholar who read an earlier draft of this book noted that by trying to understand the perspective of the believers, I'm following in the footsteps of the Harvard psychologist William James. In his 1902 book *The Varieties of Religious Experience*, James takes religious experience seriously, without accepting that there are supernatural beings. In this sense, we both (though of course I'm no William James) take "weird beliefs" seriously but not literally. I hope to shed light on the causes, form, and function of the alien-abduction belief by answering the primary questions that so many of us have. How and why does someone choose to study this phenomenon (Chapter 1)? What is the source of the abduction experience (Chapters 2–3)? If it didn't happen, then why are all the stories so similar (Chapter 4)? If it didn't happen, then why do so many disparate people believe it did (Chapter 6)?

And why is this topic important in the first place? There are at least three good reasons we should care why normal people come to believe they were abducted.

The first reason has nothing to do with aliens. It is simply that alien abductions are a "weird belief" and—granted that there are differences in the form and content of such notions—believing weird things is a very human trait and always has been, regardless of century, culture, or socioeconomic status.[12] Hence, picking one such weird belief and exploring it in depth can shed light on the mechanisms by which people develop and endorse outlandish ideas.

Second, believing weird things may prove to be harmful for the believer. Hence, understanding why and how we come to believe can serve a protective function: it can act as a prophylactic against developing the beliefs in the first place. Carl Sagan argued that science is more than a body of knowledge; it's a way of thinking— one that involves reasoning, coherent argument, rigorous standards of evidence, and honesty. And it's a method that must be *taught*. If we don't learn and practice "these tough habits of thought, we risk becoming a nation of suckers, up for grabs by the next charlatan who saunters along. . . . We can't help but fall prey to spurious accounts that snare the gullible."[13] Sagan's views find strong support from an unlikely source: political scientist Jodi Dean, who contends that in today's increasingly complex technological society, we're becoming less and less able to discriminate between truth and fiction, facts and hypotheses, science and pseudoscience.[14]

Third, understanding why people believe weird things is important for anyone who wishes to know more about people—that is, humans in general. Even if we take into account all of the factors we'll be exploring—the dearth of rational thinking, the prevalence of memory distortion, the ubiquity of culturally available scripts —we still can't explain why anyone would *want* to believe in such a thing as alien abduction. After all, being abducted is creepy; it's painful; it involves terrifying sexual and medical experimentation; and claiming to have been abducted is a sure way to be labeled daft. Why on earth would people subject themselves to this without strong reasons?

As we will see, there *are* strong reasons. Behavioral scientists have largely been tone deaf to the real purposes that such "weird" beliefs serve and the benefits they confer on the holder. For many people in Western society today, magic, religion, and faith have been extracted from daily life and replaced by an emphasis on science, on facts, on things that can be seen and measured. But what fills the gap that is left? Abduction beliefs poignantly reveal that the desire to find meaning and purpose in life is more fundamental than many of us realize.

1 How Do You Wind Up Studying Aliens?

How did I come to study alien abductions in the first place? Many abductees I've interviewed believe I was drawn to the topic because I myself was abducted. Some people think I'm excitingly open-minded, or possibly just nuts. The truth is more prosaic. I was a little lost and I walked through a back door. Originally, I had no interest in aliens or alien abductions. I was interested in memory. Also in not spending my entire life in graduate school.

I began a Ph.D. in psychology at Harvard in the mid-1990s, during the height of the "recovered memory wars." Could traumatic memories be utterly repressed and then recovered years later? The question was at the center of a bitter and volatile debate.

On one side were the trauma advocates, who believed that some experiences were so terrifying, painful, and overwhelming that they could be entirely forgotten. This forgetting, they said, occurred because of repression—a hypothesized defense mechanism that relieves the mind of pain by rendering traumatic memories inaccessible to conscious awareness. Although theoretically any type of traumatic event could elicit repression, the vast majority of reported cases involved childhood sexual abuse. Many psychotherapists, confronted with a wide range of puzzling and intractable symptoms in their patients, had come to believe that childhood sexual abuse was at their root—even if a patient could not remember that such abuse had ever happened. The therapists considered it their job to help the patient recover those memories and understand the profound trauma that gave rise to the suffering.

At the same time, skeptics—many of whom were academics—believed that the whole concept of repression was a clinical myth, unsupported by any real evidence. Most research showed that not only were traumatic events remembered; they usually were remembered *all too well.* So the skeptics believed that if patients "recovered" memories in therapy, they were probably remembering events they only *imagined* happening, under guidance from the therapist. They were creating false memories.[1]

The debate continues today. What it really comes down to is whether memory works differently for traumatic events than for ordinary ones. Those who believe in repressed memories say it does: when events are traumatic, repression and dissociation (what many people call "spacing out") set in as protection. The skeptics say it doesn't: when events are traumatic they almost always get remembered, and no special emotional memory mechanisms exist. The most recent research indicates that although some details of traumatic events may be forgotten or confused, the core of the memory—what actually happened—generally remains intact.

No debate has ever done more to tear the field of psychology apart. A decade ago, during the bitterest phase of the controversy, the skeptics labeled repression advocates as fools, while the advocates came to see skeptics as arrogant or even as apologists for pedophiles. Passions ran high, for these theoretical arguments had real-world implications. Should alleged sexual abusers—often fathers—be imprisoned on the basis of their daughters' recovered memories? Should psychotherapists encourage people with psychological problems to try to come up with what "must have" happened to them? Should the statute of limitations for reporting crimes be overturned in the case of recovered memories? Court dockets all over America were filling up with criminal cases pitting lawyers, victims, and expert witnesses against each other, with family relationships, truth and justice, and huge sums of money at stake. As more patients recovered memories in therapy, more families sued therapists for damages; as more people were sent to jail on the basis of recovered-memory testimony, more advocacy groups were formed to fight on behalf of the accused.

This was a minefield that I as a graduate student had no intention of going near. But in those days you could scarcely avoid it if you had any serious interest in psychology—or even if you didn't. Celebrities were sharing their personal abuse histories on television, and bestselling books were encouraging people to go into psychotherapy to unearth their own. So many cases of recovered memory of satanic ritual abuses had been reported that the FBI was pressured to start an investigation. (It never found any physical evidence that such ritual abuse had ever occurred.) Women who had gone into therapy were discovering, with the help of hypnosis, that they sometimes had numerous personalities, and Multiple Personality Disorder was being described as a profound consequence of repressed childhood sexual abuse. Nursery schools were being shut down and teachers imprisoned because, after lengthy and suggestive questioning, children were describing bizarre episodes of abuse, some involving flying clowns and broomsticks and the killing of large animals.

And my own psychology department was caught up in the fray. The chairman, Daniel Schacter, a leading memory researcher, argued that what appeared to be recovered memories were probably false memories, created in therapy sessions between enthusiastic psychotherapists and suggestible patients. My advisor, Richard McNally, a clinical psychologist, studied cognitive functioning in people who had been exposed to trauma. One day over lunch they discovered they both wanted to study memory functioning in people reporting recovered memories. Were such people more likely than others to create false memories in a laboratory setting? If so, the finding (while not completely disproving the repression hypothesis) would be consistent with the argument that repression did not exist and that some people were more likely than others to create false memories. It was a great idea for an experiment, and Dan and Rich needed a graduate student to help them get the job done.

At the time I was working on a study examining whether cardiac hyperreactivity was a genetic marker for alcoholism. My job was to find men with a family history of alcoholism, get them drunk on pure grain alcohol, administer a pain-sensitivity test to their right index finger, and then record their heart rates during the ascending and descending limbs of the intoxication curve (in other words, as they were getting drunk and then sobering up). This job required a unique skill set: I had to be able to mix drinks, attach electrodes, inflict pain, measure blood alcohol levels, and tactfully yet effectively slap away frisky men.

One summer morning, just after testing a subject so drunk that he didn't feel the pain in his finger and suggested I apply it to his nipples, I bumped into Rich McNally walking his dog outside the Psych Department building. Normally too intimidated to talk to him, I asked if he might be looking for another graduate student to work in his lab. When he asked whether I would be interested in spearheading the false-memory project, it never occurred to me to say no. I had definitely lost interest in cardiac hyperreactivity as a genetic marker for alcoholism. The false-memory question interested bigwigs in my department (read: highly superior intellectual beings whose support could rejuvenate my flagging self-respect); it would be relatively easy to explore with standardized laboratory methods; and it was a wholly new area of inquiry. Not only would I complete my Ph.D. in short order, but I'd get to work with luminaries in my field *and* be the first person to scientifically explore memory functioning in people with recovered memories. I felt like a fieldworker on an archaeological dig who falls into a hole and, while scrambling out, skins her knee on the lost city of Atlantis.

In a nutshell, this was the plan. I was going to recruit female sexual abuse victims from the community. I was going to look for three groups: women who had "recovered" memories of their sexual abuse, women who had been sexually abused and always remembered their abuse, and women who had never been abused at all. Then I was going to bring them into the laboratory and run them through a number of experiments that would examine their memory functioning. The experiments would all be standardized, employing methods widely used in the field.

One of the experiments involved something called guided imagery. Skeptics of repression hypothesized that some types of techniques used in therapy may inadvertently cause patients to create false memories. In guided imagery, patients who were unsure whether they had been abused were asked by the therapist to imagine what such abuse might have been like. Prior research indicated that when people in a laboratory setting were asked to imagine events in vivid detail, they were subsequently more likely to believe the events had happened. One such paradigm showed that after college students were instructed to imagine unusual childhood incidents (ones that were very unlikely to have happened, such as a situation in which they'd knocked over a punch bowl at a wedding), they became more confident that such incidents had actually occurred.[2]

I used this "imagination inflation" protocol to test whether people with recovered memories—as opposed to those with no history of abuse—were more susceptible to thinking things had happened to them after merely imagining them in the lab. Why did it matter? Because if women with recovered memories were more likely to succumb to imagination inflation in the lab, it was possible they'd be more likely to do so in the real world as well.

Another series of experiments involved a list-learning experiment known as the Deese/Roediger-McDermott (DRM) paradigm. Subjects were asked to memorize a series of word lists. Each list comprised semantically related words (such as "sugar," "candy," "sour," "bitter") all strongly related to another word (such as "sweet") that was *not* presented on the list. This unpresented word was called the "critical lure." Researchers had repeatedly found that subjects often remembered the list as including the critical lure. That is, the subjects created false memories in the lab.

I recruited women who reported sexual abuse and those with no abuse histories. If the former group was more likely to create false memories in the lab, this would be consistent with the hypothesis that they were more susceptible to false-memory creation outside the lab as well.

Didn't it occur to me that testing false-memory creation in sexual-abuse victims would be controversial? Well, I was idealistic. I believed that science was protective—that if you tested reasonable questions with sound research methods and submitted your results to the arduous peer review process, you were removed from the front lines of any controversy. I wasn't fighting; I was just collecting data. I was as neutral as Switzerland.

But getting the research done was not so simple. The fact that research and writing aren't always fun was nothing. The tough part was hearing all the stories my research subjects told me. I interviewed more than two hundred men and women with sexual-abuse histories, asking difficult questions about what exactly had happened. When? Where? How? Who was the perpetrator? The stories were heartbreaking, and I was totally unprepared for my reactions. Sometimes I started to cry during interviews and had to invent an excuse to leave the room.

I was equally unprepared for readers' reactions once I had written up the studies for publication. I'd been very careful in my methods, and I submitted the data to the peer review process—a painful experience in which people smarter than you get to attack your research anonymously.

The results of the guided-imagery paradigm were surprising: women with recovered memories were *less* prone to imagination inflation. Contrary to my hypothesis, they were not particularly susceptible to creating false memories in the lab.[3]

It was hard to interpret this finding. In contrast to the control subjects, about half of the recovered-memory subjects seemed to catch on to the purpose of the experiment. They would say things like, "Oh, I see what you're doing—you're trying to find out if you can get us to create false memories." These subjects—who were particularly concerned about the purpose of the experiment, and how the results might affect the way sexual abuse was treated and understood—were quick to see through our method (and to get ticked off). In psychological jargon, it was a "transparent paradigm." The most I could say after concluding the experiment was that vigilance against false-memory creation could perhaps protect a person from imagination inflation in the lab.

In contrast to the guided-imagery paradigm, the DRM paradigm yielded fairly clear results. These indicated that people with repressed memories *were* more likely than others to create false memories in the lab, a finding consistent with the idea that such people might be particularly likely to believe in the reality of events that they had merely read about or imagined.[4] The fact that sexual-abuse victims were prone to creating false memories in the lab could be explained in several ways. Two obvious ones conflicted with each other. Either the abuse had never occurred and the individuals had developed false memories of events they merely imagined. Or the abuse *had* occurred and was so horrific that they had repressed their memories, and this repression had led to memory impairments that manifested themselves in their lab performance.

But since my article didn't discuss the matter in sufficient detail, many outsiders concluded one thing: I believed that these people had not been abused. The phone started ringing off the hook. How could I do this to the victims of such crimes? Why was

I hurting them even more than they'd been hurt? One published letter called me "a friend of pedophiles everywhere." Not only was the public at large upset, but I was being vilified by many in my own scientific community. A trauma researcher at Harvard Medical School told a *New York Times* reporter that my research had a "political agenda."[5] Grad school friends stopped talking to me. A Harvard Medical School psychiatrist took me to lunch and over tepid baked scrod told me that I should pick another research area, because otherwise I'd be unlikely to get a job when I graduated.

Ten years later, I finally understand what was going on. The theory of repression is inextricably tied to childhood sexual abuse, and after centuries of being denied or ignored, sexual abuse was finally being acknowledged for the evil it is. A theory had been yoked to a social movement; and if I was questioning repression, I had to be questioning the existence of sexual abuse. When I said, "You're prone to creating false memories," people heard: "I don't believe you've been abused." This wasn't what I was saying, but it didn't matter. Any research looked like a threat to the progress that advocates for victims of sexual abuse had fought so hard to achieve.

Science had been sold to us graduate students not as a collection of facts, but as a process aimed at the pursuit of truth—one in which there were supposed to be no forbidden questions. Yet when it came to sexual-abuse research, this certainly was not the case.

I hated the controversy, and I hated being seen as a secret enemy of all those people who had shared their painful memories with me. But then a safer way to study the creation of false memories turned up.

After Harvard Medical School had concluded its investigation of John Mack's research methods, Mack was encouraged to apply a multidisciplinary approach to his study of alien-abduction claims. Accordingly, in the spring of 1999, he invited a group of academics ranging from astrophysicists to anthropologists to come to Harvard's Divinity School, where they brainstormed with mental health professionals and a number of abductees.[6] Rich McNally returned from the conference impressed by the conviction with which the abductees spoke about their experiences. He wanted to bring them into the lab and examine their psychophysiology as they were in the act of remembering their encounters. Did they react to scary abduction memories the same way they reacted to scary events that had actually happened? Did I want to collaborate?

I liked the idea immediately. Here was a group that had "repressed memories," but the memories would be much less painful to hear about than memories of childhood sexual abuse.

Even better, alien abductees were people who had developed memories of a traumatic event that I could be fairly certain had never occurred. A major problem with my research on false-memory creation by victims of alleged sexual abuse was that it was almost impossible to determine whether they had, in fact, been abused. I needed to repeat the study with a population that I could be sure had "recovered" false memories. Alien abductions seemed to fit the bill.

The plan was simple: find people who believed they had been abducted by aliens, get them into the lab, interview them about their memories, and then run them through some of the paradigms I had used with the sexual-abuse victims. When tested with a variant of the DRM paradigm, would abductees be more likely than other people to create false memories in the lab? Would they yield the same results as the sexual-abuse victims with recovered memories? If so, this addressed the corroboration issue (since it was certain the event hadn't happened) and provided further support for the hypothesis that people who "recovered" memories were creating false memories of events they had merely imagined.

It took three months to convince Harvard's Institutional Review Board that this was a viable research project, but at last I got the green light and ran the first of many newspaper ads seeking subjects: "Have you been abducted by aliens?"[7] By 10:15 A.M. my voicemail in-box was full.

Most of the calls were from local TV stations, radio shows, and newspapers curious to know why Harvard was interested in aliens. Some were from ticked-off Bostonians ("Doesn't Harvard have *better* ways to spend all its goddamn money?"). A few painful calls came from Latin Americans who had misunderstood the ad, and thought we were looking for illegal immigrants abducted by U.S. border patrols. One call was from an alien. It came as I was on my way out of the office for the night, and I let the answering machine pick it up. After the beep, there was silence. As I hovered in the doorway, the machine emitted a static-like sound, followed by about twenty seconds of punctuated, atonal beeping. There was an eerie syntax, almost a cadence, to the noise, and it ended with a prolonged hisssssssssss. It was no less creepy the tenth time I played it, amid a safe crowd of fellow graduate students the next morning.

But there were also calls from abductees—about fifty of them over the course of a month. I had to rule out the psychotics—the ones who called from hospitals, halfway houses, shelters, and detox units to tell me that aliens had switched their brain with that of Britney Spears. Yet a number of the callers were potential subjects. Some based their abduction beliefs on certain physical and psychological symptoms (oddly shaped moles, sleep difficulties, sexual problems); others had actual memories of being abducted; and a few suspected they might actually *be* part alien. (Usually these were young single men who worked with computers.)

At first I was delighted that the individuals were willing to speak so readily about their beliefs. The screening calls sometimes went on for an hour. I quickly learned, though, that most people just wanted someone to listen to their stories. They would invite me to go out for coffee, to come over for homemade meatballs, to watch home movies about the lights in their backyard. But they were wary about participating in a lab experiment because they weren't sure what the research might show. They worried that by participating they would expose themselves to continued denial, disbelief, and ridicule. They didn't want to have their memories "tested"—to get involved in a project that would further damage the validity of their claims. Some agreed to participate, but only if I promised not to publish any research indicating that their memories were false—a promise I couldn't possibly make. After thirty-one days of recruiting, I'd found only one abductee who was prepared to sign a consent form.

His name was Robert, and I scheduled him for a lab session at 10:00 on a Thursday morning. I expected someone who would be, well, a little weird-looking, if he showed up at all. But the guy who appeared in my office was gorgeous. He was wearing a light-gray cashmere V-neck sweater that fit him like a glove, and he looked like a well-groomed Viggo Mortenson. I had interviewed lots of research subjects: old ones, young ones, crazy ones, depressed

ones who cried nonstop, antisocial personalities who—unsolic-
ited—confessed to crimes ("The DA thought it was only assault,
but it was actually rape"). One man with obsessive-compulsive
disorder ate an entire bag of mini-Snickers in twenty minutes; a
young woman requested that all three of her personalities be interviewed; an unpleasant young man, whom I interviewed when I
was eight months pregnant, remarked: "Man, if I had you from
behind I wouldn't even know you were knocked up." But Robert
threw me completely, because he was just so . . . normal. He had
some weird memories of alien abduction, yes, but he acknowledged their implausibility. He was skeptical about what had happened to him during hypnosis and was open to other interpretations. He spoke about his experiences with an appealing mix of
self-deprecation, skepticism, humor, fear, and surprise.

Robert shattered my preconceptions about what abductees
would be like. He didn't fit into any of my stereotypes. He hadn't
played *Dungeons and Dragons* as a kid, he wasn't a computer programmer or a sci-fi buff, and he'd never attended a *Star Trek* con-
vention. He had a beautiful wife and drove a Volkswagen station
wagon. He liked to ski, watch French movies, and cook Thai food.

Not only did Robert teach me to keep an open mind; he jump-
started my research by introducing me to his network of fellow
abductees. Soon after our interview, I was invited to attend an annual weekend retreat held by a close-knit group of abductees, "believers," and paranormal researchers at an old New England inn.
The owner believed she'd seen an alien outside her bedroom window in 1976, and since then had generously used her considerable
resources to help "further the cause." This was a chance I couldn't
turn down.

And the inn wasn't the Bates Motel, either. It was a charming

Victorian mansion with a fancy swimming pool, surrounded by a manicured lawn that sloped gently down to the harbor, where a fifteen-foot Boston Whaler was tied up for guest use.

My first abductee of the weekend was Al, round and bald, with a film of sweat glistening on the top of his head. Within five minutes he had me in his room, ostensibly to show me his artwork—computer depictions of his intense alien-abduction experiences. His artwork turned out to consist of many pictures of naked women with enormous breasts spread-eagled across flying saucers, kitchen tables, and car hoods. Superimposed over the naked bodies were the kind of alien faces we've all seen—green, with black almond-shaped eyes and slits for a nose. The sort of stuff my fifteen-year-old cousin liked to find on the Web after his parents went out for the evening. Al looked at me expectantly, but I couldn't think of a single appropriate response.

I felt that way for much of the weekend. The abductees and I spent two-and-a-half days together, taking our meals in the main dining room, playing volleyball in the pool, eating ice cream cones while meandering through the town's winding streets, sipping cocktails on the porch at sunset. I spent most of the time listening. There were stories about abduction experiences (including discussions of the contrasting sexual appetites of "grays" versus "whites"), jokes shared at the expense of skeptics ("Can you believe they tried to tell us it was a flock of birds heading south?"), and lots of "remember when" tales. "Remember when Sally first started getting her memories, and she was so freaked out that she checked herself into rehab?" "Remember when Manchester Dan saw that sci-fi channel documentary, and the aliens looked *exactly the same* as the one that got him?"

At dinner the first evening, I had a long conversation with

Vivian, a thin, beaky woman dressed in flowing purple. She had recovered her memories two years before, with the help of a psychotherapist in San Francisco. Her aliens looked different from the ones described by the others. They were, she said, "Scandinavians": fair-skinned, with silky blond hair. They'd come for her in a spaceship ringed with blue lights. Before being abducted, she'd been lonely, broke, depressed—"on the verge of some kind of nervous breakdown." Afterward things had looked better. The aliens had left her with a gift—a way of telepathically communicating with them. Vivian was now self-employed as a "channeler," helping people get in touch with aliens. She felt comfortable enough with me (apparently my aura was warm) to tell me something personal: she said I was interested in this area because I myself had been abducted. Would I like to be channeled to find out more?

In the evenings, after dinner, talks were given on the patio. A shaman from South America discussed the architecture of Mayan temples and the way it indicated alien intervention: it was far too advanced (compared with other architecture of its time) to be human in origin. A computer engineer showed us a slide of the inside of an Intel computer chip and the structural layout of an Incan tomb, and pointed out their resemblances: further evidence that aliens existed. Two guys from MUFON talked about unidentified flying objects (UFOs) and the patterns of UFO sightings in the United States over the previous ten years. Such sightings, they said, came in waves: when one was reported in the media, other reports quickly followed. This they took as evidence for the reality of UFOs. A clinical psychologist who specialized in group therapy for alien abductees showed some "ground-breaking" new data. He could use Rorschach inkblot interpretations to differentiate between patients who had been abducted and patients who hadn't. I asked if he knew beforehand which patients were which. He did. His study had been rejected by three scientific journals—which showed, he said gravely, that "the scientific community just isn't ready for this."

An elderly gentleman named Budd Hopkins, a well-known abduction researcher, artist, and author, talked at length about the intense emotions that emerge during hypnosis when abductees remember what happened to them—a clear indicator of validity.

The highlight of Saturday evening was a conversation with two brothers from Manchester, New Hampshire. These men were relatively well-known abductees who had written a book about their experiences. One night in the late 1960s they'd been canoeing on a lake in Maine and had seen some weird lights across the water. A few years later, one of them had fallen down an elevator shaft at work; he'd suffered brain damage, developed epilepsy, and become severely depressed. A therapist had concluded he was feeling depressed not because he'd fallen down an elevator shaft and sustained brain damage but because "something" must have happened that night on the lake. Repeated hypnosis sessions helped him remember what it was: after he and his brother had seen the lights on the lake, he'd been sucked up through a "tunnel of light" into a spaceship and medically and sexually experimented on by a team of small gray beings. These events had subsequently been confirmed by his brother, after he too was persuaded to undergo hypnotic regression.

Mostly, I listened. I felt as though these people and I only seemed to speak the same language. We used the same words, but with different meanings. To them, "evidence" meant anecdotes ("A whole family in Pittsburgh say they were abducted together"), coincidences ("I was driving west, and I heard on the news that that's where the UFO was sighted"), ambiguous marks on the body ("Sure, the bruises could have come from the construction site, but that Strieber book said the beings sometimes leave marks"), and feelings ("Pictures of aliens scare me"). To me, "evidence" meant one thing: objective external validation. Show me an alien and I'll believe they exist.

Now and then during the weekend, I would tentatively suggest alternative explanations for the experiences I was hearing about. "Did you know," I asked Budd Hopkins, "that hypnosis puts people into a very suggestible state, in which it becomes relatively easy to confuse imagination with reality?" "Yes, I know," he said. "But that's only if it's not done correctly. I'm very careful." A woman named Ruth told me that the crucial event for her had been a nighttime episode in which she'd felt terror, been unable to breathe, and heard footsteps. I asked her if she thought the symptoms could have been related to sleep paralysis. "No—because, see, I wasn't asleep when it happened. I was on the couch watching David Letterman." She was positive she'd been abducted. A fellow named Sam attributed his impotence to the same phenomenon. I asked him whether his recent prostate surgery might not be the cause. No, he said. "I've read that stress can cause impotence."

It was clear that Occam's Razor, the principle of parsimony that underlies all scientific theory making, did not come naturally to these people.[8] For a given set of symptoms or experiences—say, "having bad dreams"—there were countless possible causes, ranging from angels to ghosts, from indigestion to bio-tech firms out to steal sperm in the middle of the night. But for these folks, abduction by aliens was the theory that best fit the data.

After everyone had spoken on Saturday night, I was asked to comment. I'd had two gin-and-tonics, and I'm very sorry to say that I went on a riff about how anecdotes do not count as scientific evidence. I pointed out that no matter how sincere and sane they all were, no matter how heartfelt their experiences, such reports are subject to error. Our perceptions are faulty! Memory is reconstructive! Hypnosis does weird things! After I'd finished, there was a long pause. Then one of the abductees turned to Budd and said, "Tell her about the metallic tube that came out of Jim's nose, the one that went down the sink before you both could catch it."

Well, this wasn't a crowd of graduate students in science. Like most people in the world, they hadn't been drilled in the application of logic, argument, rigorous thinking, and appropriate standards of evidence. They didn't understand the phrase "burden of proof"—which means that anyone who makes an extraordinary claim has to prove it, not expect others to disprove it. I, on the other hand, had emerged from my painfully expensive education with a set of mental flashcards that read, "When faced with competing hypotheses, choose the simpler one," and "Look for independent confirmation," and "Coincidence is not significant," and "Extraordinary claims require extraordinary evidence."

But more to the point, these nice people weren't interested in truth, at least not the kind of truth you find with scientific methods. Alien abductees have faith. They believe what they believe not because of any objective evidence but in spite of it. They didn't question their experiences. They were trying to confirm their beliefs.

I got a grip on myself and shut up. I wasn't there to influence their beliefs. Even attempting to do so made me feel like a grump and a party pooper.

Besides, what struck me the whole time was how normal these people were. Yes, they held some strange beliefs without any strong evidence to support those notions. But don't many of us do the same thing? They weren't much weirder than the people I see at family reunions. My relatives believe that Ireland is the seat of modern culture, that Guinness is its own food group, and that swimming off City Island in Long Island Sound is good for your health. The people I meet in Ivy League universities have their own share of irrational beliefs: that working 120 hours a week to make money you have no time to spend is a reasonable way to live; that a city dweller needs an all-terrain vehicle; that they understand how wireless computer technology works. I myself believe that strenuous exercise is a form of self-loathing and that buying shoes is an effective treatment for depression.

The truth is that almost all of us can believe things without much evidence. The only thing unique about the alien abductees I have met is their *particular* weird belief.

I didn't start out being interested in alien abductions. If it hadn't been for some bad experiences when I was trying to study memories of sexual abuse, I never would have met Robert or Budd or Vivian or any of the others, and my life would have been a little emptier. These people with their improbable beliefs taught me a lot about questioning before judging, about listening before drawing conclusions, and about how we come to believe what we do. My time in the alien-abduction community was not only eye-opening and strange; it fundamentally changed how I understand human beings. Weird beliefs become a lot less weird when you try to understand why people hold them in the first place.

2 How Do People Come To Believe They Were Abducted By Aliens?

"I once had this terrible nightmare—at least I think it was a nightmare. Something was on top of me. It wasn't human. It was pushing into me. I couldn't move; I couldn't scream; I was being suffocated. It was the worst dream I've ever had. When I told my therapist about it, she basically asked me if anything had happened to me as a kid. She was getting at sexual stuff, like if I had been abused. It took me off-guard, because I'd never thought about that before. Anyway, she said that sometimes memories that are really traumatic get pushed down by the psyche—it's like a protective mechanism—and that they can kind of 'pop up' in dreams. I didn't . . . don't think I was ever abused—actually, sex is an area of my life that I pretty much feel in control of—but she made me think. Had something happened to me? Maybe something did happen. I wondered a lot, because it seemed like my life wasn't going the way it should. Relationships were really hard for me. . . . Getting through graduate school seemed tougher for me than for other people. . . . I have a lot of trouble sleeping. It's so weird because I was such a happy kid. It was around the time I hit puberty that everything changed. For some reason, I started to have images of aliens popping into my head. Did you see that movie *Signs*—the one with Mel Gibson? The aliens looked more like those, not like the more typical ones. I'd be walking to school and then POP—an alien would be in my head. Sometimes I'd hit my fist against a wall, because then the pain would help me think of something else. I really thought I was going crazy. After a while, I told a friend—Rob. I think you spoke with him; he's a graduate student at the Divinity School. He gave me a book to read. The book was called *Abduction* or *Abductions* and it was written by a famous psychiatrist at Harvard. It had lots of stories about people who'd been abducted. I read the book in one sitting. I couldn't put it down—it all clicked with me. I knew what the people were going to say even before they said it. I completely got what they felt—the feelings of terror and helplessness. I couldn't stop thinking about the book. Once I started thinking maybe I'd been abducted, I couldn't stop. Finally I told my therapist about what was going on, and she said she couldn't help me with this, but she referred me to a psychologist in Somerville, someone who worked with people who believe in things like this. The first time I went to see him, he asked me why I was there. I opened my mouth to talk, but I started crying and couldn't stop. The tears were just pouring out of me. I'm not the kind of person who cries easily—I don't think I'm an emotional person. It was then I understood that there was something going on, that something had happened to me and I didn't know what it was. He said that I shouldn't be afraid, that this was very common, that it was the first stage of coming to realize what happened to me, that in some people the memories get only partially erased, and that those people can access them if they're willing to do the work, to undergo hypnosis and allow themselves to find out."

When I was first recruiting subjects for my study of alien abductees, I assumed that people wouldn't answer my ad unless they had actual memories of being abducted. I mean, the ad read: "Have you been abducted by aliens?" Why would you answer it if you didn't have any such memories? On what other basis would you think you'd been abducted? But as it turned out, most people who answered the ad merely *believed* they'd been abducted: in fact, they had no detailed personal memories of their abduction experience.

An initial phone screening would reveal that, yes, they thought they'd been abducted by aliens, so we would set up an interview at my office. The first question I'd ask would be, "How old were you when you had your first memory of being abducted by aliens?" "Oh, I don't have memories," they'd say. I was amazed. "You don't have any memories of the experience? Why not?"

Because, I was told, their memories had been rendered inaccessible. Some said the reason was that the aliens "erased my memories" or "the beings programmed the experience to be forgotten." A few believed (like some victims of childhood sexual abuse) that what had happened to them was simply too traumatic to be consciously available: the experience was "too awful for my mind to handle it, so I repressed it." Whatever the mechanism endorsed, the consequence was the same: there were no personal memories of the abduction.

But if they didn't have any memories of being abducted by aliens, then why did they believe they'd been abducted in the first place?

Everybody I spoke with had one thing in common: they'd begun to wonder if they'd been abducted only after they experienced things they felt were anomalous—weird, abnormal, unusual things. The experiences varied from person to person. They ranged from specific events ("I wondered why my pajamas were on the floor when I woke up") to symptoms ("I've been having so many nosebleeds—I never have nosebleeds") to marks on the body ("I wondered where I got the coin-shaped bruises on my back") to more or less fixed personality traits ("I feel different from other people, a loner—like I'm always on the outside looking in"). Sometimes they included all of the above. Though widely varied, the experiences resulted in the same general question: "What could be the cause?" In short, it appears that coming to believe you've been abducted by aliens is part of an attribution process. Alien-abduction beliefs reflect attempts to explain odd, unusual, and perplexing experiences.

This search for causes was well described by Terry, a thirty-seven-year-old elementary school teacher. "I went to dinner with some friends. We finished late and I was tired. But instead of just driving home, I felt compelled to drive south out of the city. I drove for like an hour, down Route 3, and then I turned around and came home. The next morning when I woke up, I turned on the news and found out that an unidentified flying object had been spotted south of the city, in the general vicinity of where I'd been driving."

Jon, a thirty-nine-year-old teacher, told this story: "I'd lived in the city my whole life, but moved to a very rural area in New York

State for a new job. . . . I started to be afraid of being alone, especially at night. I'd been used to peace and quiet—but not anymore. I got, like, really scared to be by myself. I wondered why."

Here's Martha, a twenty-seven-year-old preschool teacher: "About a month ago I started noticing this bruise on my thighs. I don't know what could be causing it. Every time I think it's going away, it gets dark again. It's really weird, not like a big deal or anything, but I want to know what it is."

And these are the words of a sixty-three-year-old retiree named Renee: "Let me tell you—you're a shrink—I've been in therapy basically my whole life and nothing is helping me. I've tried psychoanalysis, medication, meditation, and I still feel depressed. I've been depressed since as long as I can remember. Something is seriously wrong with me, and I want to know what it is. I want to live a normal life."

For many abductees, the "I wonder why" stage begins after a frightening sleep experience. They wake up suddenly, terrified and paralyzed, sure that something is in the room with them, or that they're hurtling through the air, or being electrocuted.

Shawna, a twenty-eight-year-old bartender and graduate student, told me: "One night I woke up in the middle of the night and couldn't move. I was filled with terror and thought there was an intruder in the house. I wanted to scream, but I couldn't get any sound to come out. The whole thing lasted only an instant, but that was enough for me to be afraid to go back to sleep."

Mike, a forty-four-year-old computer programmer said: "I woke up around three A.M. and couldn't move. I managed to open my eyes and there were creatures in the room with me. I saw shadowy figures around the bed. Then I felt this pressure like pain in my genitals. I must have fallen asleep again, because the next thing I remember it was morning. I woke up in a state of shock."

And this is how James, a fifty-year-old dermatologist, described it: "I found myself waking up in the middle of the night, seized with fear. There were beings standing around my bed, but I was totally paralyzed, incapable of moving. I felt surges of electricity shooting through my body."

Scientists have an explanation for these experiences. It's called *sleep paralysis*—a condition that occurs when our sleep cycles become temporarily desynchronized. Instead of moving seamlessly between sleeping and being awake, we find ourselves in a limbo where the two states briefly overlap.

When we sleep, certain neural mechanisms block motor output from the brain to the rest of the body, so that we're essentially paralyzed. This is important, because otherwise we'd be thrashing around, talking, shouting, and lashing out violently in our dreams.

But when sleep cycles overlap, it's possible to "wake up" before sleep paralysis has waned. If this happens, we'll be unable to move. And if we wake up while we're in the process of dreaming, dream material might linger into our waking state. We can find ourselves hallucinating sights, sounds, and bodily sensations. They may seem real, but they're actually the product of our dreams.

Despite the bizarre symptoms and effects, sleep paralysis is considered normal, not pathological. About 20 percent of the population has had a least one episode of this type, accompanied by hallucinations. We are particularly prone to such experiences during periods in which our normal sleep patterns get disrupted. People at risk include night-shift workers, travelers with jet lag, parents with newborns, and academics trying to finish grant applications. Though it takes only about a half a minute for things to return to normal—for the perceptual, cognitive, and motor aspects of the sleep cycles to become resynchronized—this can seem an awfully long time to the victims. It is a truly frightening experience.[1]

That sleep paralysis is "normal" might be comforting to those affected if they knew what it was. Almost no one does. There are no public-policy programs to raise awareness of its existence, no feature articles in major magazines. Doctors don't mention it during checkups, and it's never been the topic of a talk show or popular book.

That being said, a *lot* of people in the world experience sleep paralysis, feel the urge to take long drives at night, are afraid of being alone in rural areas, find weird bruises on their bodies, have unexplained nosebleeds, or feel out of place in society. All of us at some point in our lives have symptoms, feelings, or experiences that we don't understand—but not all of us wonder deeply about them. This might be because we either don't care very much or don't think our experiences have a specific cause. Indeed, some people remain unconcerned in the face of anomalies that would perplex even the most complacent types. ("Yup, I got this rash all over me. Doc said it's something called purpora, pigmented purpora. . . . Nope, don't know how I got it. . . . Nope, not sure when it's going to go away. . . . Contagious? Don't think so. . . . What is it? I already told you, it's purpora!"). But this isn't the case with abductees. For them, what happened *is* meaningful and they want to know the cause.

The search for meaning is the catalyst for alien-abduction beliefs, but this quest hardly makes abductees unusual. Thinking about oneself, trying to understand why one has certain disturbing or baffling emotions, is a cultural preoccupation, and finding causes for personal experiences and feelings is a major industry.

Open the phonebook and look at the lists of counselors, therapists, homeopaths, psychologists, and psychiatrists. Walk into a
bookstore and check out the section on self-help and psychology.
Some people believe that if they understand *why* they feel the
way they do, they'll be able to change things for the better. Others
are greatly relieved to learn that their problems are caused not by
their moral failings but by a psychological syndrome or a little-
known disease.

But when there are so many available explanations—from ex-
cess carbohydrates to parental neglect, from insufficient Bikram
yoga to too much Prozac—why pick alien abductions? What
makes abductees unusual is not the perceived strangeness of their
experiences, or their desire for explanation, but *the specific explanation they choose.* Why do some people come to believe that their
sleep paralysis experiences, or their nighttime urges to take long
drives, or the strange marks on their body are caused by extraterrestrials?

The answer is that their symptoms, feelings, and experiences
are consistent with what they already know—or "know"—about
alien abduction. In America today, few people are unaware of
what aliens look like and what they supposedly do to the human
beings they kidnap.[2] Since the 1960s we've been hearing widely
publicized stories of alien abductions.[3]

According to the standard script presented in books, TV shows,
and movies, aliens come in the night. When they approach you,
you cannot move. You feel terrified and helpless. You levitate, feel
vibrations running through your body, see shadowy figures. It's
common knowledge that aliens leave strange marks on your body,
such as bruises or scoop marks; that UFOs are seen at night from
solitary cars on wooded roads; that when you've had an encounter

with extraterrestrials, you're unable to account for a period of time; that afterward you feel anxious or depressed, different from other people and from your former self. For better or worse, alien abduction is one of our culturally available explanations for weird experiences like sleep paralysis and gaps of lost time. In Chapter 4 we'll look at the historical process by which this happened—how "I've had an encounter with aliens" went from being a sure sign of insanity to the subject of prime-time TV shows *(Mork and Mindy, Third Rock from the Sun, Roswell),* bestselling books *(Communion, Abduction),* blockbuster movies *(Alien, Predator, Close Encounters of the Third Kind, Men in Black, Signs),* and allegedly serious documentaries.

When you're looking for the cause of an anomalous experience, your search is limited to the set of explanations you've actually heard of. For most of us, the set of possible explanations is far from complete. We're unaware of the prevalence of sleep paralysis, sexual dysfunction, anxiety disorders, perceptual aberrations, chemical imbalances, memory lapses, and psychosomatic pain. But our set of possible explanations does include alien abduction, because everyone knows about aliens and their modus operandi (they come in the night, fill you with terror, kidnap you, and erase your memories). "What happened to me is just like what everyone else says happened to them." "I'm not really into science-fiction stuff. Before this happened, I never believed in aliens. But what I saw on that TV show is exactly like what happened to me."

Look at things from the perspective of forty-year-old Mike, who's had a frightening episode of sleep paralysis. He thought he was going to die. He's never had an easy time sleeping, and now he's absolutely terrified. He *has* to know what happened to him. Some possible explanations occur to him: he's going crazy; he eats too much before going to bed; there are robbers in the house; he has brain cancer; he saw something supernatural, like ghosts or aliens. He's not sure. Okay, the supernatural explanations are unlikely, but the other ones just don't seem "quite right. . . . They don't fit what happened. . . . It was unlike anything that ever happened to me." Days later, browsing through the remainders in a local bookstore, he sees a book entitled *Communion,* by Whitley Strieber. He leafs through it and discovers, on page 27, that the author once had a sleep experience just like his. And just like him, Strieber was freaked out and was afraid to go back to sleep. And just like him, Strieber always had a tough time sleeping, and relating to women, and figuring out what he wanted to do with his life. And it's a published book! A bestseller! Nonfiction! Mike buys it and keeps reading, and then, in a later chapter, he finds out that Strieber was prone to headaches and nightmares as a kid, just like him. All these coincidences are too much. Did what happened to Strieber happen to him? Could he have been abducted by aliens?

Another one of my abductees, twenty-seven-year-old Larry, had a weird dream in which he saw shadowy figures standing around his bed. He woke up with a stabbing pain in his genital area. It was a "terrifying experience." Familiar with *Close Encounters of the Third Kind* and other movies about aliens, he wondered if he might have encountered extraterrestrials. Upon reflection, however, the shadowy figures seemed to him "too tall—I don't think aliens are that tall." Next, he considered the possibility that the groin pain stemmed from a repressed memory of childhood sexual abuse. He began to review family photo albums in an effort to retrieve memories of what might have happened to him. Because of the groin pain, the feeling that he was "somehow special, differ-

ent from other people," and the "stealthy nature" of the experience, he briefly wondered whether a high-tech bio firm in the area
had sent employees into his home to take sperm samples, but he
quickly dismissed this as being "too unlikely." He considered the
possibility that the experiences were spiritual in nature, but "I
doubt that angels would wear hoods." He tentatively settled on
the childhood sexual abuse explanation. Only after undergoing
therapy and failing to recover memories of childhood sexual
abuse did Larry conclude that he had been abducted by aliens.

Someone else I interviewed, a man named Paul, forty-one, was
working for a resort in the Caribbean when he had two strange experiences. In one, he woke up naked on the couch, but he couldn't
remember either lying down there or undressing. In the other, he
dreamed he saw a small creature by his bed wearing a silver track
suit, and he told the creature: "I hate what you're doing to me."
After these experiences, he started to feel "vulnerable" when he
went to bed. He stopped sleeping naked. He described himself as a
"New-Agey" guy who believed that "Western science is very limited in its understanding of the universe; I'm open to things other
people might not accept as being real." He had read widely about
"past lives, ESP, spirits, and extraterrestrials." He also told me
that he was very interested "in earth spirits that feature in native
folk tales." He considered each possible cause, but "the only explanation that seemed to fit" was aliens. "I hear that they come
into your bedroom and take you, and when they put you back it's
in a different place."

According to Jon, the teacher mentioned above, "Trouble sleeping could have a lot of causes. It could be stress. It could be that
I'm not used to the new place yet. It could be something worse,
like being contacted by aliens. Yeah, it sounds crazy, but who

knows? The world is a weird place. . . . There's a lot we don't know. . . . I've been stressed before, but I haven't had trouble sleeping."

So people choose alien abduction as an explanation because they can. In the words of retiree Doris, seventy-three, from New Hampshire: "Why else would I wake up flying over my bed?"

"But it's so unreasonable!" one hardcore skeptic said to me. "There's no evidence that aliens even exist, never mind that they actually come to our bedrooms at night!" While this is true, it's not clear that the average person knows just how little evidence exists for extraterrestrial life, or just how improbable visits from extraterrestrials are.

For most people, reports by other individuals count as evidence, especially if those others appear sane, attractive, and respectable. Betty and Barney Hill—the mom and pop of abductees —became famous in abduction history in the 1960s because, in the words of Seth Shostak, an astronomer associated with the SETI Institute, "they were more or less Mr. and Mrs. Front Porch."[4] A number of equally sane, attractive, and respectable people have since produced bestselling books and popular screenplays about their abduction experiences, and many people view this large body of testimony as powerful evidence.[5] But because the scientific community disagrees, abductees gripe that "scientists don't pay attention to our experiences."

For a scientist, anecdotes don't count as evidence. A thousand individual eyewitness reports are no more meaningful than one. This is because humans are fallible, and even with the best of intentions we have limited knowledge and we all make mistakes. What we "think we saw" may not be what we saw at all. So from a scientific perspective, the only good way to validate a claim is to do so objectively. How do we know that earth is round? Because the earth's shadow on the moon is round, because photographs from outer space show that the earth is round, because a ship's topmast is the last thing you see as the ship sails off toward the horizon.[6] We don't know the earth is round because your boss's cousin, who's a very respectable guy, said so. If anecdotal evidence or the words of attractive authorities could be relied on, we'd have to accept that Yeti and the Loch Ness Monster exist, that Elvis Presley, James Dean, and Jimi Hendrix are alive, that psychoanalysis cures schizophrenia, and that there were weapons of mass destruction in Iraq at the time of the 2003 invasion.

It's interesting that people seem to find anecdotal evidence compelling when the issue is alien abductions, but not when the issue is, say, murder. Perhaps this is because there have been so many recent TV crime shows (such as CSI: Crime Scene Investigation Las Vegas and its offspring, CSI: Miami and CSI: New York) that clearly demonstrate what types of evidence are required to convict a suspect. In these shows, people get convicted on the basis of sperm samples, blood spray patterns, body temperature, and the type of bug crawling in the victim's nasal cavities, not because of what "Bob told my cousin Helen, and she never lies."

The possibility that aliens exist, and that they visit the earth, doesn't seem all that implausible to many people. In fact, it seems quite probable. According to recent polls conducted in the United States, about 94 percent of respondents said they thought that intelligent aliens exist. In a more recent poll, conducted by CNN, 65 percent of respondents thought that UFOs had actually visited Earth.[7]

In the words of eighty-three-year-old Joe, a retired construction worker, "I think ETs must exist. There are so many planets. . . . No reason to think it's just us out there. Hell knows, there's nothing special about us. Scientists don't know everything. No one can prove they don't exist. And it would make sense that something else is out there. Some kind of God, or something above us. . . . I like the idea that there's something magical out there. I have this buddy, and when he's had a few beers he talks about what happened to him. He was driving to Vegas one night and he saw something. A light in the sky. It followed him. He blacked out— and when he woke up, the car was in a ditch. He had no memory of what happened. Like I said, he don't talk about it much, but when he does he thinks something happened to him. He thinks something's going on. Why else would all these people be talking about it? Why all the movies, and books and all that? Where's there's smoke there's fire I always said. And all those books written by military people. . . . I'm not saying anything for sure. I'm just saying there's a lot going on out there that people don't know about. What do we think—that we're alone out there? Then where do we come from? The Big Bang they talk about—well, what about before that? And everyone gets worked up about how they're taking people in secret, through walls. Why do we think that ETs, if they exist, would have the same laws of gravity or biology or whatever? Maybe another kind of being or life exists, one we can't even imagine. Anyway, all I'm saying is that anything is possible and that there must be something going on for all these people to be saying the same thing. Attention, the wife says— they're doing it to get attention. But who the fuck (pardon my language, little lady)—who the fuck would want to have that happen to them?"

Many people would agree with some or all of what Joe says, but there are a lot of problems with it. For one thing, the "sheer number of planets" argument overlooks the fact that no matter how many planets there may be, they have to be hospitable to life, and, as we know just looking around at our own solar system, the right environment is not easy to come by. Is a certain planet just the right distance from its sun? Does it have the right temperature? Is there any water? Is it dense enough to support an atmosphere? If we consider all the prerequisites for life, this drastically reduces the number of planets available.[8]

But let's say that some other type of life *does* exist somewhere in the universe. What are the odds that it evolved far enough to be intelligent? Evolution is opportunistic and unpredictable, and there's no inexorable path from one-celled organisms to intelligent, self-aware life. In fact, ninety-nine out of every one hundred newly arising species become extinct. Earth is a planet hospitable to life, and life did arise here. Since then, more than a billion species of animals have come into existence, yet only one possesses conscious intelligence. Humans *are* a miracle.

But let's say, for the sake of argument, that self-aware intelligent life *did* exist elsewhere in the universe. Why would those beings develop the fantastic technology they would need to get here across interstellar distances? Moreover, why would they want to? Why would such superior beings be interested specifically in us? Why would they be interested in egg harvesting and sperm sampling? Why would they be taking the same bits and pieces of people over and over again? The whole idea of aliens coming to earth in UFOs and kidnapping humans for medical and genetic experimentation is not only extremely unlikely—it's downright silly. (Especially the part where the aliens wait nervously while you're getting undressed.)

But like many of us, believers don't think in terms of probability, and don't habitually look for the simplest explanation. I al-

ways asked the abductees I met, "Do you think there's a better explanation for what happened to you?" And in essence they always
answered, "Maybe—but I trust my gut and my gut says aliens."

Even if people did know how to think probabilistically and parsimoniously, would they? Even if they understood that anecdotal
reports don't count as evidence, that the probability of alien life is
infinitesimally low (never mind alien life that defies all known
laws of physics, biology, and chemistry to abduct you from your
bedroom and mate with you), would they think any differently?

I doubt it. Lots of crash courses in scientific thinking might
whittle down the number of people who "believe," but believers
would still exist. When people are sorting through possible explanations for their anomalous symptoms and experiences, especially emotionally powerful ones, they rely not on abstract principles of parsimony or probability but on what "seems to fit" or
"feels right" or "makes emotional sense."

Schizophrenia researchers know this. For almost a century
they've been trying to understand how patients form delusions.
In psychopathology the term "delusion" refers to a false belief
that is strongly held despite outside evidence and that is entirely
resistant to disconfirmation. Delusions are, along with hallucinations, one of the hallmarks of psychosis (colloquially referred to
as "being crazy"). That being said, there is a good deal of disagree-
ment in the field about what precisely constitutes the difference
between a delusion ("I am the new Messiah") and a strongly held
idea ("I have been abducted by aliens"). Brendan Maher, one of
my teachers, used to say that "if the hair stands up on your arm"
while a person describes what he believes, then you're probably
dealing with a psychotic. Textbooks suggest that one can distinguish delusions from nonpathological beliefs according to the de-

gree of conviction with which individuals hold to their beliefs despite clear contradictory evidence. One noted researcher on hypochondriasis taught that the distinction could be made on the basis of whether the individual is willing to entertain the notion that he might be wrong about his belief.

Today "delusions" are generally understood as patients' best explanations for the odd sensory and perceptual experiences that are part and parcel of their disorders. According to this perspective, delusions reflect not disordered thinking, but normal thought processes that people engaged in to explain their perceived abnormal experiences (that is, why they feel the way they do). Brendan Maher offered a memorable example in his "Psychopathology of Delusion" course at Harvard. He described the case of a woman who believed she had a hive of bees buzzing and stinging in her head; she complained about the bees for years. After she died, an autopsy revealed a brain tumor. It was the tumor which had almost certainly caused the weird sensations of buzzing and stinging that she'd felt and, quite naturally, tried to explain.

Though I was impressed with this theory of delusions—that they were people's explanations for their anomalous experiences—one thing bothered me. Why did the explanations have to be so weird? Why did the woman in Maher's example speak of a beehive and not "side effects from a neurological condition that is impairing my sensory and perceptual systems"? Why would someone say, "The CIA is after me," rather than, "I'm losing my hearing"? I remember Brendan Maher looking at me across the room, smiling patiently, and saying, "Because that's what it felt like to them."

For a long time, I didn't really understand what he was talking about. But today, thanks to the alien abductees, I do. (Though I'm far from suggesting that alien abductees tend to be psychotic or otherwise psychiatrically impaired, they do hold false beliefs—ones that appear to be natural by-products of their attempts to explain the unusual things that have happened to them. So in that sense, research on the psychopathology of delusions extends nicely to nonpathological beliefs like alien abductions.) It baffled me that most of my abduction subjects had considered and rejected alternative explanations, ones that were more reasonable and more probable than an explanation based on aliens. Why choose the outlandish explanation? Given all the available explanations for sleep problems, depression, and sexual dysfunction, why choose the weird and disturbing one, the one that was likely to stigmatize them and cost them their friends?

My interviewees answered this question for me and confirmed what Brendan Maher told me ten years ago. Robin, a lovely and intelligent twenty-one-year-old college student said it best. "I know you think it sounds weird. Everyone does. I do too. But what you don't understand is that I know the abduction was real, so it doesn't matter what you think. What I felt that night was . . . overwhelming . . . terrifying. . . . There was something in the room with me. All I can say is that it happened to me, it didn't happen to you. . . . I felt them. Aliens."

What emerges again and again from the subjects' statements is that what happened to them *felt* alien. It didn't feel as if it could be explained in conventional, ordinary, mundane ways.

As Maher and others have argued, delusions (false beliefs) are people's best attempts to explain their anomalous experiences.[9] And the vividness and immediacy of personal experience cannot be easily refuted. Assuring abductees that what they believe happened is infinitely unlikely, that there is no evidence to support it, is a waste of time. They have a different, more compelling kind of evidence: first-hand experiences are *real*. Any experience is accompanied by and dependent upon neural activity. Although neural activity is normally the *consequence* of external input, it can be created by direct activation of the neural substrate itself. Regardless of the source, instances of neural activity can all feel the same.[10] Hence, the only way to distinguish between a "feeling" that an abduction occurred and its objective reality is through objective corroboration—something that in the case of alien abductions just doesn't exist.

So what are the kinds of things that feel so weird to abductees? Let me try to make this argument less abstract. As already described, sleep paralysis is an internally generated experience that is often attributed to something external: aliens. This is because it feels really creepy. Imagine this happening to you:

After watching the evening news, you wash your face, brush your teeth, and go to bed. In the middle of the night, you suddenly wake up. You're wide awake. You open your eyes and try to get up, but you can't. You're on your back, completely paralyzed. There is a sinister presence in the room. Then you hear something. Footsteps? Something is padding softly through the room. Your heart is pounding and you try to scream, but you can't. Whatever is in the room moves closer. Then it's on top of you, crushing your chest. You glance to the left and see small shadowy forms in the corner. Your muscles are clenched and you're aware of electric sensations shooting through your body. Then the sensations stop. . . . The experience passes and you can move again. Your heart rate slowly subsides and you begin breathing normally.

*   *   *

What the hell just happened? This is what most people who've had such an experience want to know. It's definitely what I wanted to know the first time it happened to me. And I had just written a paper on the topic! Although the phrase "nonpathological desynchrony in sleep cycles" kept running through my head the whole time, this certainly didn't alleviate the disorientation or the terror or the gasping for breath. The physicality of it was overwhelming.

It was an episode of sleep paralysis, an experience that's been scaring the living daylights out of people for centuries.[11] And for centuries, normal people have been looking for an explanation outside themselves. A sensed presence, a shadowy creature moving about the room, a strange immobility, a crushing pressure, and a painful sensation in various parts of the body have been historically compatible with a host of improbable explanations. The phenomenology of the experience may be the same, but explanations differ depending on what the individuals—and the larger culture they live in—believe, expect, or infer could be possible. At other times and other places in the world, such night terrors have been interpreted as Satan, demons, witches, dragons, vampires, large dogs and angels and erect gorgon. Today, it's extraterrestrials.

Yet although it's true that—phenomenologically speaking—sleep paralysis and alien-abduction experiences have a lot in common, there is one important difference: sleep paralysis is a fact; alien abduction isn't. So if you wake up in the middle of the night levitating above your bed and spinning like a chicken on a rotisserie, you should understand that the experience is roughly a billion times more likely to have been caused by something normal than by something paranormal. But be careful about telling this to an actual abductee.

Susan: You know, it's interesting. The experiences of sleep paralysis and contact with aliens have a lot in common. But the thing is that sleep paralysis is a well-documented medical experience, and so far as we know there's no evidence that aliens exist. Don't you think that your experience is much more like likely to have been caused by sleep paralysis?

Abductee: No!

Cell phone conversation overheard through the door a few minutes later: I'm totally pissed. Can you believe the nerve of that girl? She comes to me, like, "Oh, I believe you've been abducted! Let me interview you to learn more about the phenomenon!" And then she brings up this sleep paralysis shit. "Oh, what really happened is sleep paralysis." Riiight! How the fuck does she know? Did she have it happen to her? I swear to God, if someone brings up sleep paralysis to me one more time I'm going to puke. There was something in the room that night! I was spinning. I blacked out. Something happened—it was terrifying. It was nothing normal. Do you understand? I wasn't sleeping. I was taken. I was violated, ripped apart—literally, figuratively, metaphorically, whatever you want to call it. Does she know what that's like? Fuck her! I'm out of here!

You can't disprove alien abductions. All you can do is argue that they're improbable and that the evidence adduced by the believer is insufficient to justify the belief. Ultimately, then, the existence of ETs is a matter of opinion, and the believers have their own opinions, based on first-hand experience. They are the ones who had the experiences that require explanation. They are the only ones who can tell us which explanation seems to fit best.

All of the subjects I interviewed followed the same trajectory: once they started to suspect they'd been abducted by aliens, there was no going back. (I have no idea what the turning point might be for those who start to believe and then are convinced otherwise. This would be an interesting area of research. Perhaps it would shed light on psychological and cognitive factors that are prophylactic against creating false beliefs.) Once the seed of belief was planted, once alien abduction was even suspected, the abductees began to search for confirmatory evidence. And once the search had begun, the evidence almost always showed up. The confirmation bias—the tendency to seek or interpret evidence favorable to existing belief, and to ignore or reinterpret unfavorable evidence—is ubiquitous, even among scientists. Once we've adopted initial premises ("I think I've been abducted by aliens"), we find it very difficult to disabuse ourselves of them; they become resilient, immune to external argument. We seem to be habitual deductivists, rather than inductivists, in our approach to the world. We do not simply gather data and draw conclusions; instead, we use our prior information and theories to guide our data gathering and interpretation. Once abductees have embraced the abduction theory, everything else tends to fall into place. Alien abduction easily accommodates a great variety of unpleasant symptoms and experiences. It can explain anything and everything—"I always had nightmares as a kid," "I had a troubled adolescence," "I'm not interested in sex," "I've been having stomach pains," "I keep failing rehab." One subject, who was part alien, finally found an answer to a life-long question: "I look at my mother and I think to myself, 'I don't know you. Who are you?'"

Furthermore, once you believe, your belief becomes unfalsifiable. There is no way to prove that aliens *don't* exist. All you can do is argue that there's no evidence they do, that their existence is improbable. Abduction beliefs fall into Karl Popper's category of unfalsifiable propositions. These may be *scientifically* meaning-less—but we don't live in a science lab. We live in the real world. In the real world, people don't ask whether there is enough evidence to justify their beliefs. They ask: What are the costs and benefits? Believing in aliens might cost them some friends. Relinquishing their belief would cost them a lot more. They would have to find another explanation and cast aside a compelling theory for their scary and unpleasant symptoms and experiences.

Nowadays when skeptics say to me, "People must be really nuts to think they've been abducted," I disagree. First of all, coming to believe one has been abducted by aliens doesn't happen overnight. It's a gradual process. It progresses in fits and starts, through many stages, in which the possibility comes to seem more and more believable. Second, as we shall see in Chapter 3, very few people are dead sure they've been abducted by aliens until they "get their memories." After that—well, if you had vivid memories of being sucked up into a tube of light, you'd probably be sure too. Third, all people want to understand why weird and confus-ing things happen to them; for better or worse, alien abductions have become one of the explanations culturally available to us. Fourth, very few of us are trained to think probabilistically and parsimoniously—and even if we were, we *still* couldn't refute belief in alien abduction. Finally, abductees generally entertain a num-ber of possible explanations before embracing the theory of alien abduction. The reason they ultimately endorse abduction is ac-tually quite scientific: it is the best fit for their data—their per-sonal experiences. And skeptics can't critique those data, because they have no access to them.

Abduction beliefs are natural by-products of our attempts to explain the unusual things that can happen to us. Given that most of us want to understand our feelings, that very few of us think like scientists in our everyday life, and that alien abduction is a culturally available script, I often wonder why more people don't think they've been abducted. Today, confessing to such a belief doesn't make you "crazy"—it just puts you, in my opinion, a couple of standard deviations from the norm. Ten years from now, believing in aliens and in their presence among us will perhaps become as common as believing in God.

3 Why Do
I Have
Memories
If It Didn't
Happen?

Joe was thirty-four, single, and college educated—a tall, pale, skinny, soft-spoken man wearing jeans, a baggy black sweater, and red Converse high-tops. He was an artist who earned a living as "a technical-support guy for a computer company—I work the graveyard shift so I can be in the studio during the day." When asked about his religious background, he said: "I was raised a Catholic, but I don't believe there's any one religion. People should feel free to practice what feels right to them. I don't go to church, but I do consider myself a spiritual person."

About two years before our interview, Joe had had a number of disturbing sleep-related experiences. "I would wake up in the middle of the night terrified, like I'd been having a nightmare. My heart was pounding and I was really scared. I tried to yell for help, but I couldn't because I couldn't move. . . . I felt like something was in the room watching me, but all I could see was the gray shapes." Afterward, "Of course I wondered what caused it. . . . I figured it was a really weird dream, or stress because of the new job. . . . Something related to stress, maybe."

One night, a few months after one of these nighttime episodes, he was watching TV. "There was a movie on about a family that had been abducted—in Canada, I think it was. . . . In the movie one of the characters—it was the father—had the same thing happen to him that happened to me. He woke up and couldn't move. He was, like, paralyzed or something. And then in the morning he didn't remember what happened. In the movie, it was related to contact with extraterrestrials. . . . I knew it was a just a movie, but still it was interesting that our experiences were exactly the same."

A couple of weeks later, Joe found himself in a local bookstore. "I was looking in the science section to see if there was anything interesting on the universe, life in the universe, stuff related to that." A girl who worked in the store recommended a book by "a pretty famous abduction researcher at Harvard. . . . It was about the alien-abduction memories that some of his patients had under hypnosis." After Joe had read this book, he went online to find out more about the author and his work. During his search, he stumbled on a website for abductees. "There was a checklist that you could fill out about symptoms that alien abductees report. . . . I filled it out, just for the hell of it. I ended up checking off almost all of them."

At this point Joe did not "necessarily believe the whole abduction thing," but he was becoming increasingly "struck by the coincidences." "And I have to admit, the whole idea of aliens is fascinating to me. . . . I mean, who knows? The universe is immense. Why do we believe we're alone?" In a Web chat room frequented by people who were interested in the topic of extraterrestrial life,

Joe met a girl and they eventually started dating. She thought it was possible Joe had been abducted, "because I fit the profile. . . . She's very, very intuitive. She just felt like there was something I didn't know about myself."

About two months after they started dating, Joe visited the office of an abduction researcher he'd located on the Web. "I still didn't really believe anything had happened to me. I just wanted to talk about how I was feeling and try to understand why I was getting preoccupied with the idea." After an initial talk, Joe agreed to undergo hypnosis. "I wanted to get some help remembering what had happened on those nights, . . . to see if something else might have happened that I don't remember."

In the first session no memories were retrieved, but Joe wound up crying. "I couldn't stop, and I don't think I'd cried since I was about five." In the second session, he "recovered" memories of his abduction by aliens. In one of his first memories, he was strapped down on a black marble table. An alien standing to his right, with "menacing black eyes," forced a device like a suction cup onto his genitals. Sperm were sucked painfully out of his body. "It was the worst terror I've ever felt. I was helpless, in pain. It was violating. It was like the worst dream I've ever had, only worse. I can never forget that image, and I will never be the same person again."

Joe was normal. He was nice. He was in a healthy relationship, with a stable job, and recently he'd even sold some paintings (peaceful Vermont landscapes). How does someone like Joe end up convulsing on his therapist's floor as he recalls such horrific experiences?

*   *   *

In contrast to Joe, most of the abductees I spoke with never actually had any memories of their extraterrestrial experiences. Most of the people who called in response to my ads simply *believed* that they'd been abducted. They weren't necessarily *sure.* They believed because such an event seemed to fit the pattern of feelings, symptoms, and experiences (sleep paralysis, depression, erectile dysfunction, and so on) that preoccupied them.[1]

That being said, they did not all hold their beliefs with the same degree of confidence. Though I didn't attempt to quantify the differences in degree during the data-collection process, there seemed to be a continuum of confidence. At one end: "Could I possibly have been abducted?" At the other end: "I was abducted." The latter group comprised about 10 percent of the abductees who called in response to my ads. Why were they so confident? For a good reason: their belief was not based solely on symptoms and feelings. They had detailed and terrifying memories of what had happened to them.

Why do some believers acquire memories and others do not? That question is at the heart of this chapter. It so happens that most of them either sought out or fell into the hands of an abduction researcher or therapist (sometimes they were the same person), someone who used certain psychotherapeutic techniques that he or she believed would help abductees retrieve their lost memories or fill in the sketchy details of the ones they had ("I saw a light and I don't remember anything after that").

These techniques go by different names (hypnosis, guided imagery, regression therapy, relaxation therapy, energy work), but they all work in roughly the same way: the therapist lulls the abductee into a suggestible state, in which normal reality constraints are relaxed, and then asks the abductee to vividly imagine things that might have happened. Of course, it *is* possible to create memories of alien abduction without the use of such a technique. Some people can do it on their own—they are good at imaginative role-playing. One of my subjects reported that she'd read a book about alien abduction and had begun to imagine that the experiences she'd read about had happened to her. After a few weeks of imagining different abduction scenarios, she had dreams in which "they came true." And a few weeks after her dreams, she developed detailed memories of being abducted and experimented on by aliens, "just like I read about in Whitley Strieber's book."

But although it's possible for some people to develop memories in the absence of imaginational therapy, this is uncommon. Most of my subjects who had abduction memories—like most subjects in the scientific literature who report such memories—acquired them through hypnosis or other related psychotherapeutic techniques. For example, of the eleven that agreed to participate in the memory study discussed in Chapter 1, eight had their memories emerge under hypnosis (two underwent other techniques to recover memories, and one recovered them after watching a TV show about aliens).

We shouldn't be surprised that abductees looking for memories to underpin their beliefs and fears end up in hypnosis. Most abduction researchers, as well as most books and movies about alien abductions, present hypnosis as a reliable method for retrieving memories. As we'll see in the next chapter, the earliest published accounts of alien abductions—subsequently made into TV movies and feature films—showed abductees recovering memories with the aid of caring and concerned professionals using hypnosis. John Mack, the most widely known researcher, declared: "Hypnosis appears to complete or greatly add to the process of remembering and has proved in this field to be a valuable therapeutic and investigative tool."[2] Hence, most abductees who have recovered their memories have done so after hypnosis, which they underwent in the first place because the idea of undergoing hypnosis to retrieve memories is pervasive in our culture, represented in countless books, movies, TV shows, cartoons, and websites.

What is hypnosis, and how does it work? Many people believe, with the encouragement of overenthusiastic therapists and dozens of fanciful movies—from *The Manchurian Candidate*, *The Three Faces of Eve*, *Agnes of God*, *Stir of Echoes*, *Curse of the Jade Scorpion*, and *Identity*, to, most recently, *The Butterfly Effect*—that hypnosis can enable you to recall things you can't remember otherwise. The implication is that hypnosis is a kind of psychological truth serum: take it and you'll have no choice but to reveal secrets of the past, hidden in the recesses of your unconscious mind.

This belief is wrong. A wealth of solid research, conducted over four decades, has shown that hypnosis is a bad way to refresh your memories.[3] Not only is it generally unhelpful when you're trying to retrieve memories of actual events, but it renders you susceptible to creating false memories—memories of things that never happened, things that were suggested to you or that you merely imagined. If you (or your therapist) have preexisting beliefs or expectations about "what might come up," you're liable to recall experiences that fit with these beliefs, rather than events that actually happened.[4] Worse, neither you nor your therapist will realize this, because the memories you do retrieve *seem* very, very real. To debrief an abductee, said psychiatrist John Mack, is to be "in the presence of a truth teller, a witness to a compelling, often sacred, reality."[5]

How does this happen? What is hypnosis, and how does it render a person susceptible to false-memory creation? Hypnosis has been defined—in a rather circular way—as a social interaction in which an individual experiences anomalies of perception and memory that have been suggested by a hypnotist.[6] These experiences do not correspond to objective reality. The subject may hallucinate objects that aren't there, or may fail to perceive sensory stimuli. Hypnosis can thus be quite useful in certain circumstances.[7] As a college student, I was lucky enough to work with the famous researcher Martin Orne at the University of Pennsylvania. He used hypnosis to help inner-city kids cope with the pain caused by sickle-cell anemia. But just as hypnotic suggestion can distort and alter the experience of pain, it can distort and alter memory.

Since the late nineteenth century, there has been lots of controversy over the precise nature of hypnotic effects. In a nutshell, the main issue is: Are the hypnotic effects *real,* or is the subject making them up? The question is hard to answer—we have no way of knowing for sure whether a subject's report is faithful to his or her subjective experience.

There are a handful of experts in the field who debate the topic vigorously. I have no interest in joining this tempest in a teapot. I don't have the towering IQ you need to compete—and even if I did, I still wouldn't care very much about the precise nature of the mechanisms that are at work in hypnosis. What matters is that, regardless of what the mechanisms are, hypnosis has been successfully used to create false memories. One oft-cited paper supporting this fact was published in *Science* in 1983. Two researchers at the University of Waterloo in Canada hypnotized twenty-seven subjects and then suggested to them that they'd been awakened one night the previous week by some loud noises. After coming out of hypnosis, thirteen of the subjects stated that the suggested event had occurred; and six of these thirteen were *absolutely certain* the event had occurred. Even when they were told that the hypnotist had suggested it to them during hypnosis, these subjects still maintained that they'd been awakened by loud noises. Said one subject, "I'm pretty certain I heard them. As a matter of fact, I'm pretty damn certain. I'm *positive* I heard those noises."[8]

An important caveat: research seems to indicate that it is not hypnosis per se that causes the false memories. These can develop in any situation in which misleading information is conveyed to participants and their imaginations are stimulated.

Overestimation of the unique power of hypnosis is possibly linked to the idea that hypnotic phenomena are produced by an altered state of consciousness. Yet despite more than seventy years of effort, researchers have been unable to find any markers of a hypothesized "hypnotic state," and still cannot say whether the brain scans and behavior patterns of a person who's in a hypnotized state differ in any way from those of a person who's just deeply relaxed.[9] If the phrase "hypnotic state" is used at all, it should be nothing more than a shorthand way of saying that someone is responding to suggestions made after a therapist has led him into a relaxed and responsive frame of mind.

There's no special hypnotic state that can force people to reveal the secrets hidden in their unconscious. This will be a blow to many avid fans of Hollywood movies and to bumptious psychotherapists. All that happens is that subjects respond to suggestions given to them by a hypnotist. Hypnosis encourages fantasy and imagination. Participants adopt a lax standard for distinguishing fantasy from reality probably because they *believe* they're under the influence of something like a truth serum.

In sum, decades' worth of research indicates that hypnosis can render people susceptible to creating false memories. This is in large part because it both stimulates the imagination and relaxes reality constraints. ("Yeah, this memory feels weird. I can't believe these things are coming out of my mouth, but I guess that this is what happens when you're hypnotized.") And in such situations, we become unusually susceptible to suggestions—those that are made to us both explicitly ("Did the alien examine your vagina?") and implicitly ("What did you feel after you saw the strange lights?"). Such suggestions can powerfully influence our memories.[10]

But just as a mountain of research associates hypnosis with false-memory creation, it also indicates that hypnosis per se is not what causes false memories; these can result from any technique or situation that—like hypnosis—stimulates the imagination and relaxes reality constraints. (For example, some abductees in the literature recovered abduction memories during guided imagery, "energy therapy," and massage therapy. One I interviewed had recovered hers during an intensive yoga session, and another "after smoking a bowl or few with some friends.") I concur with Robert Baker when he minimizes the importance of abductions recalled without hypnosis: it is not all that surprising that some people can "recover memories" without it.[11] Elizabeth Loftus, one of the world's foremost memory researchers, has studied many cases in which people have developed memories of traumatic events that never actually occurred. The individuals used a variety of reconstructive strategies to shape their memories; but the key to generating false memories, Loftus argues, is the protracted imagining of an event in the presence of authority figures who encourage belief in and confirm the authenticity of the memories that emerge.[12] This is what happens when abductees seek out or fall into the hands of abduction researchers who help them "recover" their abduction memories.

I can say with great confidence that if you're not a believer already (at least to some extent), you're not going to acquire memories of alien abduction. No one goes to bed totally uninterested in aliens and wakes up screaming, "Oh my God, I was just abducted by aliens!" Belief precedes memories because developing detailed, personal memories of such an experience requires intervention on the part of some kind of therapist or abduction researcher, and you won't seek out such a person to help you "find your memories" unless you already believe it's possible.

And although I think there's a positive relationship between conviction in the belief you were abducted and the probability of acquiring memories (after all, the more convinced you are, the more likely you'll be to look for someone to help you confirm it with memories), this is only a rough rule of thumb. Some of my subjects believed strongly that they'd been abducted but they never developed any actual memories. Josh, for instance, didn't want to undergo hypnosis, because he was afraid of what would emerge: "I'm not sure I can handle the truth." Others scarcely believed at all, yet still developed memories. A case in point was David, whose massage therapist suggested abduction as a possible explanation for his chronic tension and insomnia. Conveniently, an abduction researcher worked in the same clinic as the massage therapist, and David was able to go from the room where he got the explanation to the room where he recovered memories—all in one day.

Imagine a leafy plant: this is the alien-abduction belief. Now imagine a fertilizer: this is a memory retrieval technique, such as hypnosis. Regardless of how robust this species of plant becomes, it won't grow fruit unless you fertilize it. The fruit is the alien-abduction memory. Since there are always differences in soil fertility, some plants of this type need a lot of fertilizer in order to blossom, while others need just a little. But regardless of the plant's health and the composition of the soil, you probably won't get any buds at all without the fertilizer. And *with* the fertilizer, you could end up with some really strange fruit.

I was hypnotized once, by a fellow graduate student. Now, I'm generally a very sensible, practical person. I score low on measures of suggestibility, creativity, hypnotizability, and proneness to fantasy. I don't get overwhelmed by beautiful music or vivid colors or chocolate éclairs. I don't get caught up in novels or movies, and, to my mind, spectacular sunsets are merely pretty. So being the skeptic that I am, I was giggling as the fellow student instructed me to imagine a fire and then dance around it. After I'd danced awhile, he said something about my being eight years old.

And there I was—on the playground at Page School, wearing a purple Bubble Yum T-shirt, racing around with the red flag I'd captured from enemy territory, followed by a gang of children screaming, "Get her—get chicken legs! She has the flag!" I had no idea why I'd thought of this particular experience, and I had no idea why I was crying: "I hate it when they call me chicken legs! I hate being chased like this—I feel afraid!"

Had this ever actually happened to me? It must have. The details were so striking. The purple shirt was so vivid. The emotions were so real. I'm not the weepy sort, but my face was wet with tears.

I was so embarrassed by my reaction that I told everyone I knew—so that if they heard about the episode, they'd hear it from me first. My sister was kind enough to remind me that, in the first place, I'd never owned a purple Bubble Yum T-shirt (though a family friend who worked for the company had once promised to give me one), and, in the second place, we'd never played Capture the Flag until we moved to Boston—years after we'd attended Page School.

With the help of a neophyte hypnotist, I—a skeptical and not especially imaginative person, with no particular set of expectations or beliefs—had created a vivid false memory in about five minutes.

Hypnosis and other memory retrieval techniques cause false memories not only because they render you suggestible—and thus liable to be biased by your expectations and beliefs and those of the hypnotist—but also because they require that, in your suggestible state, you *vividly imagine* things that might have happened. Memory researchers have known since the work of Sir Frederic Bartlett in the 1930s that "the appearance of a visual image is followed by an increase in confidence entirely out of proportion to any objective accuracy that is thereby secured."[13] Visualizing things, imagining things that didn't happen, is an excellent way to start thinking they did.

Your ability to distinguish between things that actually happened to you and things you merely imagined hinges on your ability to recall information about the source of the memory—how, where, and when you acquired it. Memories of real experiences tend to contain perceptual details about the setting in which the knowledge was acquired ("I read it on the cover of the *Daily Star* as I was standing in the checkout line"), whereas memories of internal events, generated by imagination, fantasy, and imagery, typically do not include such details. So when you find yourself in a situation where you know something (say, that aliens examined people on black tables) but can't recall anything specific about the context or setting in which you acquired the knowledge ("Did I see this on *X-Files?* Read it in *Communion?* Hear about it from a friend? Picture it in my mind?"), you lose the basis for determining whether it is a function of "real" external experience or something internally generated.[14]

Let me make this idea less abstract. Did you spill a bowlful of punch on the bride at a wedding when you were a kid? Probably not. On a five-point scale, if 5 is "Very confident that this happened" and 1 is "Very confident it didn't happen," most people check off 1. Now I want you to imagine it happening. In detail. For five minutes I'd like you to close your eyes and imagine it happening, step by step. What did the punch bowl look like? Where was it? What did the bride's dress look like? Did it have a train? Was there lace on the train and on the sleeves? What color was the punch? Research indicates that even a rudimentary visual exercise like this leads people to feel more confident that the event they've been visualizing actually happened.[15] This is true because in situations where the perceptual clarity of an imagined event is high—where we have provided contextual details by vividly imagining the event—we have a lot of trouble distinguishing between products of reality and those of fantasy. When vivid details are attributed to imagined events, they become very difficult to distinguish from real ones.[16]

In 2004 an interesting research report was published in *Psychological Science.*[17] Though a great many experiments had shown that vividly imagining things can lead to false remembering, this study was one of the first to present neural evidence of this relationship.

It used magnetic resonance imaging (MRI) to scan the brains of subjects as they were engaged in the experimental task. The more vividly the subjects imagined a specific object (as measured by activity in the precuneus lobe and the inferior parietal regions of the cerebral cortex), the more unsure they became as to whether they had imagined it themselves or had previously seen pictures of it. These findings show that the incidence of reality-monitoring errors (errors in making distinctions between actual and imagined events) is liable to increase when the brain is engaged in visual imaging, producing visual representations that may resemble those that would have been produced if the object had actually been seen. Or, to put it another way, brain activity reflecting the engagement of visual imagery can lead to falsely remembering something that was only imagined.

Very few people believe or assume or care that they might have knocked over a punch bowl at a wedding. Still, if they spend five minutes imagining perceptual details of such an incident, the likelihood they attribute to the event will increase. What they imagined comes to seem more real to them. It seems real to their brains as well. Imagine how much *more* real it would seem if they already suspected, assumed, or believed that they'd upset the punch bowl and that it had caused an enormous uproar.

Hypnosis encourages false memories because it preys upon a memory system that is vulnerable to begin with. It amplifies our existing tendency to distort memories. Most people don't understand just how fallible memory is. As recently as twenty years ago, neither did many memory researchers. Back then, it was fashionable to say that memories of past events were like computer files: you placed them neatly in storage in your brain, and they stayed there until you wanted to pull them out again.

Today we know that memories can be messed up in lots of ways. (So can computer files, for that matter.) It's possible to perceive an event differently from the way it occurred ("There was someone in the room, and he was black"). Even if you perceive the event correctly ("It was a gray shadow") that memory can be enormously influenced over time by intervening events ("My god, that little gray alien in the movie is exactly like the thing I saw in my room that night!"). And finally, memories can be influenced when you try to get access to them ("I want you to remember back to that night—was the alien holding anything in its hand?").

All these biases come into play during hypnosis. You're asked to remember back to a sleep paralysis episode that you may not have processed correctly. Then, whatever you did remember is sure to have been distorted over time by your growing abduction beliefs, inferences, and expectations. Finally, whatever you remembered *before* you went into hypnosis will be altered by what happens during hypnosis.

The critically important point is this: our brains engage in an act of construction when we call up our memories. There's no single place in the brain that contains a "memory chip" of an experience. Instead, when we try to recall an experience, a reconstruction process begins. Various parts of the brain that have held on to disparate aspects of the memory work together, and what emerges from this reconstruction—your memory—is not the same as what actually happened. A memory is not an exact photograph of an event. It is created out of the cues that elicited the memory and the fragments of the original experience that were stored in the first place.[18]

This is a creepy idea, and many people understandably resist it. Our memories constitute who we are. They inform our personal history, our life stories, our sense of ourselves. Our lives, after all, are only what we remember of them. It's unnerving to realize that our stories, feelings, memories of the past are reconstructed over time, and that we make up history as we go along.

In 1992, after graduating from college, I moved to Colorado to find myself. I remember those years as the best of my life. When a friend recently asked me about my happiest memory, I didn't have to think twice. I immediately recalled a day in Aspen. It was my day off, there were three feet of new powder on the slopes, and I'd gone skiing with my new boyfriend, a gorgeous Australian ski instructor. It was late afternoon. We had just skied off the back line, and we were on the roof deck of his condo in a hot tub. It had started to snow, and big, beautiful, fat flakes were melting in his golden blond hair.

When she heard this story, my friend laughed and told me to pick another field to study. Why? Because she'd been there. She reminded me that I hadn't been having so much fun. I'd been wearing the wrong skis for powder and had spent most of the day falling down; the boyfriend had kept yelling, "Quality air time, dude!" every time he hit a mogul; and I'd been coming down with the flu. I hadn't really wanted to be in the hot tub; I'd had to be at work at six; and my borrowed bathing suit had been saggy and kept filling up with bubbles. It hadn't even been snowing.

She was right. The truth came flooding back to me. In the intervening years, I had distorted my memory. Snuggling with a ski instructor in a hot tub after a terrific powder day is the kind of memory I would like to have. It's consistent with my image of what I used to be (or what I wish I had been), and with what I would expect to have as a best memory. A moment of perfection in my life history was shattered by some inconvenient facts.

Other people—members of my family, for example—are much less troubled by the reconstructive nature of memory. Brendan Maher, Harvard professor, old-school gentleman, and participant-observer of Hibernian life, was the first to introduce me to the concept of the Irish Fact: "a fact-like statement that while not actually true is demanded by the flow of the narrative."[19] It's a fact that is probably not true but ought to be. As a relative of mine is fond of saying, "I made it up but I believe it's true." I grew up with the Irish Fact. Classic family stories, hilarious and outrageous, have been passed from generation to generation. It is said that Donny Murray, after imbibing a pint or two, decided to spirit away his high-school girlfriend from her dorm at St. Mary's by hijacking the fire truck in Billy Flannigan's yard and hauling her out the window. Supposedly, he dragged the wrong girl kicking and screaming out of her room, and then had to help evacuate a whole dormful of hysterical women screaming, "Fire! Fire!" Is this true? Who knows! It should have happened. With each retelling, it becomes more and more real.

What we've come to realize is that just about all people, whether they're Irish or not, have a weakness for Irish Facts. Many of us think that faithful copies of experiences are kept in the mind and reappear later in their original form; Ulric Neisser, a cognitive psychologist, called this the "reemergence hypothesis." But we really remember only bits and pieces of our experiences. When we try to reconstruct past events, we're in the position of a paleontologist trying to determine what a dinosaur looked like on the basis of a few scattered bones. "Out of a few stored bone chips we remember a dinosaur," wrote Neisser.[20]

But even if we accept that memory is fallible and that what we remember might differ from what actually happened—that our memories have been influenced by our beliefs, inferences, and expectations about what happened—it is still hard to believe that *entirely* false memories can be created. In the words of one exasperated student, "What the hell sort of bone chips get used to create an abduction memory?"

The bone chips vary according to the abductee. They're usually fragmentary memories of movies, TV shows, books, and magazine articles about aliens, things people have heard from other people about aliens, and frightening experiences like sleep paralysis. In the course of their lives, believers have collected a good deal of information on what aliens supposedly look like, act like, and do to people. They've also had numerous experiences in which they felt terror, helplessness, confusion, sadness, and pain. They no longer have "source details" about most of this information; it's just become assimilated into their lives.

Under hypnosis, people who wonder if they were abducted are lulled into a suggestible state and asked to imagine what *might have* happened. If you already believe that abduction is possible, you won't need much evidence to justify your belief that it occurred. In the context of this readiness to believe, any mnemonic experience that emerges, no matter how loose or diffuse, is likely to be taken as convincing evidence of abduction. Shards of movies, TV shows, books, articles, past emotions, imagined fears—all get pieced together into a memory. Though the construction is wobbly, the conviction isn't. Under hypnosis, abductees have trouble "source monitoring"—that is, they're prone to confusing products of their imagination with reality. In a sense, the memory that forms under hypnosis is accurate, since it does refer very generally to a real experience ("It was dark"; "I was afraid"). But it also contains many details that arise from source-monitoring errors, rather than from actual experience.[21]

My dim view of the utility of hypnosis in uncovering memories is shared by several professional societies, including the American Medical Association and the American Psychological Association. Research has confirmed over and over again that the memories retrieved, however convincing or detailed, can be bizarrely inaccurate. Courts in most states do not admit hypnotically refreshed memories as evidence. Advanced training programs in psychology and psychiatry do not teach hypnosis as a means of refreshing memories.[22]

So why is it practiced? Why do about one fourth of practicing psychotherapists use some kind of guided imagery, hypnosis, or free association to retrieve memories? Why did roughly half of the psychotherapists surveyed in a 1994 poll say they believed that memories produced during hypnosis are more accurate than those that emerge without it?[23] Why are there so many abduction researchers who are happy to use it, and so many people willing to undergo it?

One reason is that the scientific evidence on hypnosis is not reaching many of the practitioners and the general public. I know of no movies or TV shows in which a hypnotized subject remembers witnessing a murder and reports it to the police, and the police laugh hysterically because it was last week's *CSI* episode.

Another reason is that alien abductees have read or heard that hypnosis is an integral component of "getting your memories." "She told me that her memories were buried until she started undergoing some kind of guided imagery." "I read that this guy, some doctor at Harvard, can use hypnosis to help you find out what happened." It's hardly surprising that abductees believe this, since influential abduction researchers do endorse the use of such techniques. According to John Mack, hypnosis "is an essential tool in overcoming the amnesia" of abductees. Another writer and well-known abduction researcher, David Jacobs, says: "Hypnosis is integral to making sense of what happened."[24]

The routes that people take to hypnosis therapy are numerous and varied. "A friend in my yoga class told me about the interesting research this guy named John Mack was doing. . . . I decided to get in touch with him." "At the end of the book, there was a list of information resources. One of them was MUFON. I called the number and talked to this really nice guy who referred me to a therapist in New Hampshire." "I got on the Internet, did a Google search for alien-abduction stuff, and found the website of a woman in New York." "I went to a conference—it was called 'The Scientific Search For Alien Life.' On the first day, I met an amazing woman who had a support group for people who thought they'd been abducted."

Once the person locates a "specialist" and makes an appointment, what follows isn't rocket science. He or she is instructed to relax—lulled into a loose, calm, trance-like state (for me, it's remarkably similar to taking Dayquil with a martini). Then the therapist offers suggestions. "Think back to that evening and describe what happened." It's at this point that people often get hit with their first memories.

There's usually no narrative structure to these initial memories; no clear, coherent story emerges. The memories don't come all at once, or even in a way that makes sense. It's very different from what happens in the movies, where the hero doesn't know who he is or why he's in Paris with three passports and a suitcase full of cash, until he's hit on the head and the past comes flooding back. Initially, memories come in the form of terrifying images and bizarre vignettes. The person needs time to weave together the chronology and narrative structure of what happened.

"All of a sudden I saw shiny black eyes. Then I was lying on a table, back arched, with gleaming silver instruments nearby and bright lights shining down on me." "In my first energy session, I was asked to relax and was put into a trance state. . . . What was weird is that I was expecting to see my grandmother abusing me and instead, all of a sudden, I see a ship hovering outside my window. . . . I see creatures walking toward the house."

Allen, a thirty-six-year-old abductee, underwent hypnosis, and in one of his first memories he saw "a creature outside the window—huge black eyes, pointed chin, inverted teardrop head . . . no nose, naked, no color to him . . . backlit in blue." He started to scream. "It's like monsters are coming to get me, but they're real!" He was then floated outdoors to a spaceship with lots of blue light emanating from it. "I was bathed in lights—red, white, and bluish lights. . . . Then I was lifted onto a ship that had a dome on top. . . . Holy shit! . . . There was a laser beam and it went through the center of my forehead. Excruciating pain. I saw a black obsidian table. . . . There was a glass wall with humans suspended in the center. . . . I saw semen being manually extracted from my penis by alien hands—cold clammy, nonhuman hands!"

A fifty-two-year-old freelance writer named Mike sought help in trying to understand what had happened one night in Maine when he'd woken up in the middle of the night and seen a bright light. The hypnotherapist asked him to relive the episode, and he described the recall experience for me. "Oh my god! . . . I saw the light. . . . Then I was in a tunnel-like structure . . . shaped kind of like an accordion. . . . I saw beings . . . silhouettes, no real form to them. . . . They were surrounded by a huge wash of color and it was difficult to focus on them. . . . I had an image of an alien sticking a needle into my testicle. . . . I found myself screaming out loud, 'I hate what you're doing to me!'"

As these initial memories are being recalled, the terror can become so overwhelming that the experiencer can't go on. An abductee named Terry screamed, "No, stop it! I hate it!" She was too afraid to continue until the therapist had her imagine that instead of *her* entering the spaceship it was a "puppet-spy." Mike told me that in the beginning he'd sobbed, panted, writhed, and screamed.

For some abductees, the initial memories are apocalyptic confirmations of their worst fears and suspicions. "I knew it—I just knew it had happened. I felt it in my bones." But for others, the initial memories are better described as "apocryphal"; these people question the "reality status" of their memories. In the words of one such abductee: "After my first regression, I wondered if I was making it all up. . . . I still don't remember it like a real memory, like I remember walking to class yesterday." Another said: "I'm worried this is just maybe a figment of my imagination—like a manifestation of my fears or, even worse, my secret desires."

> *Abduction researcher:* Did you experience anything else being done to you?
> *Abductee:* Oh yes—there was a metal instrument, maybe about a foot long, that was inserted into my nostril.
> *Abduction researcher:* But that would have gone into your brain!
> *Abductee:* Yes, that's what it was supposed to do. The examiner came around and he had this thing in his hand and it had, like, a handle on the end. It was this long flexible thing, and he kind of leaned over my right shoulder and he wasn't looking at me. He was looking at my nostril, and he put it in as far as it could go. I didn't like it, because I couldn't breathe

very well. And then he hit something in the back and he just kind of pushed it, and he pushed it through whatever it was. [*Now sobbing*] I could feel something breaking in my head. . . . I'm wondering what they broke. . . . I don't know the anatomy, but he broke something to get it through, to get into my brain. . . . Now the examiner is looking into my face. . . . He's scrutinizing me. . . . It's like they're trying to figure out what else they need to do. They're very, very big. Their eyes—much bigger than others, and they don't blink, and they're kind of slanted on his head . . . all black, no pupil. . . . What's so disturbing about these eyes is that I think maybe it was because they didn't care. . . . Just, like, scientific, a kind of curiosity. . . . The feeling is one of total helplessness. I'm scared because they don't care about me, and I have no control over what's happening and what's going to happen.

After one of her hypnosis sessions, Terry questioned the reality status of her memories. She wondered if they could be confabulations. "I still don't remember it like a real memory, like I went to work yesterday. . . . Yet it doesn't seem like a dream. It seems more real than a dream, but not as real as me talking to you."[25]

Eventually, Terry became convinced that her memories were real. They just felt too real not to be. "I thought I was making it up until I started crying. . . . I don't think I'd be sobbing for no apparent reason, if there wasn't something there." More than one therapist has said that such strong emotions are what persuade patients of their memories' validity: "A kind of decisive indication to Catherine that she was dealing with something that was in some way real was the power and authenticity of her emotions for which she could find no other source."[26]

This leads us to the third reason I believe that hypnosis continues to be practiced: memories that emerge *feel* real—too real to be the product of suggestion and vivid imagery. Memory researchers may know that it is wrong to rely on an emotional reaction as an indicator of mnemonic accuracy, but try telling this to the person who had the reaction. Memories elicited under hypnosis feel real. And we don't have to accept only the abductees' word for it when they say they feel powerful emotions as they remember their abductions. Laboratory data confirm it. My colleagues and I, led by Rich McNally, recorded the heart rate, sweating, breathing, and muscle tone of abductees while they recalled their abduction memories. Not only were the physiological reactions of abductees similar to those of documented trauma victims, such as combat vets and rape victims; in some cases, they were even more extreme.[27]

The alien-abduction memories that emerge under hypnosis generate intense emotions—pain, terror, helplessness, awe. And these emotions then become, for the experiencer, a criterion of mnemonic validity. Abductees are not alone in making this connection: a long line of theorists in psychotherapy have argued that only accurate insights and information will resonate with a patient. So if a patient comes to feel passionately that he or she was abused as a child, many therapists consider it good judgment to accept the abuse allegation as true. So why isn't this the case with alien abductions? If people say they think abduction is the best fit for their feelings and memories, why don't we accept it?

We don't accept the alien-abduction explanation because there's no external evidence to support it, whereas there's lots of evidence to support other explanations, such as sleep paralysis and false-memory creation. But even when abductees acknowledge that sleep paralysis and false-memory creation are more probable explanations, intellectual reasoning can't alter the actual experience they had. To them, their nocturnal experiences were far too frightening to have been generated by a hiccup in the sleep cycle, and the memories they recovered in therapy were far too intense to be dispassionately described as "products of memory distortion."

Like many of us, abductees are committed to the authority of subjective experience as a means of knowing about themselves and the world. Personal experience has an immediacy, even a kind of sanctity, that scientific explanations completely lack.

Dostoevsky suffered from epilepsy. During one of his seizures, he had an overwhelming and deeply moving experience in which he felt God's presence. "The air was filled with a big noise and I tried to move. I felt that heaven was descending toward the earth and that it had engulfed me. I have really touched God. He came into me, myself; yes God exists, I cried. And I don't remember anything else." Although Dostoevsky knew that his visions were caused by epilepsy, he never stopped insisting on their validity and on the joy, truth, and knowledge they gave him. "You all, healthy people, can't imagine the happiness which we epileptics feel during the second before our fit. Muhammed, in his Koran, said he had seen paradise and entered it. All these stupid, clever men are quite sure he was a liar and a charlatan. But no, he was a victim of the disease, like I was. I don't know if this felicity last for seconds, hours, or months; but believe me, for all the joys that life may bring, I would not exchange this one."[28]

An internal, physical condition caused Dostoevsky's intense religious experiences. But that didn't stop him from feeling something external to himself: the presence of God. It didn't matter to him that "stupid, clever men" might say the feeling was due to a seizure. He believed he had felt God, and was profoundly moved and changed.

A psychologist who studies emotion once asked me, "Why don't you just tell abductees that things which feel real aren't always real?" She mentioned the phantom-limb phenomenon, the well-documented fact that patients who have had limbs amputated can still feel pain in their missing arm or leg. "Most amputees accept the fact that there's a neuropsychological basis for their problem," my friend pointed out. "They don't go around saying 'I have two legs' when they've got only one."

But the phantom-limb phenomenon doesn't work like alien abductions. For one thing, even though amputees who are missing a leg may feel sensations as if they had two legs, most of them don't claim to have two legs. Why? Because they have sufficient evidence to refute the belief: they can see, with their own eyes, that they're missing a leg. Abductees are not confronted with such a compelling refutation. And in the absence of external evidence, an emotional reaction is difficult to resist as a gauge of validity. Moreover, the phantom-limb phenomenon is, neuropsychologically speaking, well understood, luckily for the amputees. Today, no one belittles them or denies their subjective experiences. If we didn't have clear understanding of the phantom-limb phenomenon, we'd probably think the amputees were crazy too.

When abductees say, "Don't try to tell me it didn't happen—I'm the one who experienced it," I understand what they mean. Something real did happen to them. A mental experience is, after all, a real thing; it does represent a physical event in the brain. But just because you feel something extraordinary—even if it corresponds to a documented neural experience—doesn't mean that it was caused by something external to you, something out there in the world. Truth needs to be independently established rather than assumed—no matter how real it feels.

4 Why Are Abduction Stories So Consistent?

Recently, I was interviewed for a TV show on the search for extraterrestrial life. My interviewer had a Ph.D. in chemistry from a prestigious university. He grilled me for two hours about my false-memory research, asking tough, incisive questions dealing with its methods, design, and relevance to alien-abduction claims. I realized too late that I was talking to a believer. After multiple touch-ups of my sweaty face by a sympathetic makeup guy, my interviewer told me he had one more question. He said he'd left it for last because it was the most difficult for skeptics to address.

I waited nervously, mentally reviewing the list of possible questions. Had something happened that I didn't know about? Had scientists discovered a habitable planet in some other solar system? Maybe canceling my subscription to *Nature* had been a mistake.

"If, as you believe, alien-abduction memories are actually the product of false memories and thus not real, how do you explain the fact that reports by abductees from all over the United States are highly consistent, even among people who have had no contact with each other?"

I felt both relieved and annoyed. This question gets asked all the time. Still, I have a hard time answering it—not because it's compelling evidence for alien abduction, but because it just doesn't make sense. Abduction reports are *not* consistent with one another.

In the past few years, I have become a reluctant scholar of alienography. I believe I've read every account of alien abduction ever published, and just about everything that social psychologists, psychoanalysts, postmodernists, journalists, physicists, biologists, and ex-military personal have to say about them. In addition, with the help of some enthusiastic film school students, I've watched nearly every American movie and TV show ever made about aliens.

And you know what I found out? First, alien-abduction reports are only broadly similar; in their particulars, they're very different from one another. They vary enormously in details such as how people get "taken" (through walls; sucked up by beams of light; ushered into UFOs), what the aliens look like (tall; short; pads on their fingers; suction cups on their fingers; webbed hands; nonwebbed hands), what they wear (nothing; orange overalls; silver track suits; black scarf and cap), what type of examination is done (needles stuck in nose; intestines pulled out; anal "nubbins" inserted; feet examined with manicure scissors), what type of sexual activity ensues ("he mounted me"; "a rotating ball massaged me"; "my eggs were taken"; "she was beautiful, with cherry-red pubic hair"; "sperm was sucked from my penis by a machine"), what the purpose of the abduction is (human colonization; hybridization; education; communication; world destruction; world peace), why people get chosen ("I'm very intuitive"; "we're all abducted"; "I'm the chosen one"; "they wouldn't tell me").

People who claim that abduction reports are consistent either have never heard first-hand accounts or have never listened carefully. The only thing similar about abduction stories is the *general plot:* an unsuspecting ordinary human gets kidnapped by extraterrestrial beings for medical examination or sexual experimentation. All the other elements—cast, makeup, wardrobe, lines, special effects—are as different as the individuals who tell the stories. Although there are some consistent details—big heads, wraparound eyes, reversible amnesia, probing needles—both the details and the general plot existed in the movies and on TV before people ever reported personal knowledge of them.[1]

This takes us to the second thing I learned about alien-abduction reports: they began only *after* they were featured on TV and in the movies. Abduction accounts did not exist prior to 1962 (UFOs did and aliens in space did, but aliens coming to Earth to abduct humans did not). Some abduction researchers will disagree: "I've worked with people who were abducted as children! That would have been in the 1930s!" This may well be the case, but those people didn't remember what had happened to them in 1930 until they underwent hypnosis *three decades later.* Aliens with big heads and eyes were following a predictable script—abducting people, medically and sexually experimenting on them, sticking needles in them, erasing their memories—in the movies and on TV long before individuals started saying that these things had happened to them.

The third thing I can say about alien abductions is that although they are a product of the second half of the twentieth century, preoccupation with aliens is not. From the beginnings of recorded history, people have wondered about the possible existence of extraterrestrial life. In the thirteenth century, the scholar Albertus Magnus wrote: "Since one of the most wondrous and noble questions in Nature is whether there is one world or many, . . . it seems desirable for us to inquire about it."[2] And we always have. The Greek philosopher Epicurus believed that life existed elsewhere in the universe: "There are infinite worlds both like and unlike this world of ours. . . . We must believe that in all worlds, there are living creatures and plants and other things we see in this world."[3]

Between the flowering of Greek civilization in the fifth century B.C.E. and our world of today, people have written thousands of books, essays, and scientific papers about whether inhabited worlds exist elsewhere in the universe. Michael Crowe, a historian and philosopher of science, has exhaustively reviewed this body of work and concluded that the majority of educated people since about 1700 have accepted the idea that life may exist elsewhere in the universe.[4]

Why this belief in the possible existence of extraterrestrials? Well, it makes sense. The late eighteenth-century German astronomer Johann Bode defended it from a theological point of view: "Who would doubt their existence? The supremely wise creator of the world, who assigns even an insect its lodging on a grain of sand, will certainly not permit . . . this great mass of suns to be empty of creatures, and still less of rational inhabitants who will readily and gratefully praise the author of life."[5] The physicist Lee Smolin reasoned that lack of evidence proves nothing: "The argument for the nonexistence of intelligent life is one of the most curious I have ever encountered; it seems a bit like a ten-year-old child deciding that sex is a myth because he has yet to encounter it."[6] Other scientists and philosophers through the centuries have believed that our corner of the cosmos can hardly be unique. Carl Sagan called this the "assumption of mediocrity": the notion that "our surroundings are more or less typical of any other region of the universe."[7]

Some writers have believed in the possibility of extraterrestrial life; others have gone so far as to speculate about what it might look like. The Pythagoreans of ancient Greece (sixth century B.C.E.) may have been among the first to venture such speculations. According to Pseudo-Plutarch's *Placita Philosophorum* (Opinions of the Philosophers; second century C.E.), the Pythagoreans believed that "the moon is terraneous, is inhabited just as our earth is, and contains animals of a larger size and plants of a rarer beauty than our noblest efforts. Its animals in their strength and energy are fifteen degrees superior to ours and emit nothing excrementious; and its days are fifteen times longer."[8]

The fifteenth-century German humanist Nicholas of Cusa, like Johann Bode, believed that God had engendered life throughout the universe: "Rather than think that so many stars and parts of the heavens are uninhabited and that this Earth of ours alone is peopled (and with beings perhaps of an inferior type), we will suppose that in every region there are inhabitants, differing in nature by rank and attributing their origin to God, who is the center and circumference of all stellar regions." But he went further than Bode in trying to imagine the qualities those inhabitants might possess: "In the region near the sun, there exist solar beings— bright and enlightened denizens, and by nature more spiritual than those that may inhabit the moon (who are possibly lunatics), while those on Earth are more gross and material."[9]

Two centuries later, the French writer Bernard Le Bovier de

Fontenelle created a sensation with his *Entretiens sur la pluralité des mondes* (Conversations on the Plurality of Worlds; 1686), a work praised for being scientifically informed without being either boring or unintelligible to the ordinary reader (a rare accomplishment). His object was to popularize the astronomical theories of Descartes, and he did it with delightful inventiveness. He describes the Venusians as "little black people, scorched by the sun, witty, full of fire, very amorous, . . . even inventing masques and tournaments in honor of their mistresses." The inhabitants of Jupiter, he declares, are "phlegmatic. They are people who know not what it is to laugh. They take an entire day's time to answer the least question . . . and are exceedingly grave."[10]

In the United States, scholars of every stripe have wondered about life on other planets. The astronomer Percival Lowell, like many other people, believed that there were canals on Mars. He went so far as to speculate that they had been built by giant Martians who were "endowed with a highly intelligent mind and possibly possessing invention of which we have not dreamed."[11] Carl Sagan was known to speculate about the thought patterns of alien beings. He is quoted as saying: "The mere detection of an extraterrestrial radar signal [would provide] an invaluable piece of knowledge: that it is possible to avoid the dangers of the period through which we are now passing. . . . It is possible that among the first contents of such a message may be detailed prescriptions for the avoidance of technological disasters."[12]

In short, the idea of extraterrestrial life has been sparking the imaginations of remarkable people for centuries. Otherworldly beings have been represented in a great variety of ways, but they have shared one important trait: their intellectual and spiritual superiority. For as long as we've been imagining aliens, they have been better than we are.

But it's one thing to believe in and try to picture aliens, and quite another to have personal contact with them. I believe that the earliest report of communication with aliens dates from the eighteenth century and appears in the writings of Emanuel Swedenborg. Seen as a madman by some and more generously by Kant as the "arch-visionary of all visionaries,"[13] Swedenborg became famous when he was transformed from scientist to mystic after undergoing a series of religious experiences (which some have hypothesized were due to temporal-lobe seizures). Of the many theological works that flowed from his altered mind, one of the earliest was the *Arcana coelestia* (Celestial Arcana; 1749–1756). Scattered through it are sections recounting his conversations with the inhabitants of each of the planets in our solar system, as well as with those of the Moon. Among his observations: "Lunarians speak very loudly from the abdomen—from some collection of air they have there. The reason for this is that the Moon is not surrounded with an atmosphere of the same kind as that of Earth." The inhabitants of Mercury, he said, had excellent memories, "a faculty in which they excel." He frequently included references to the horses, cows, and goats of other planets, and expounded on the characteristics of aliens—their moral and mental characteristics and forms of social organization.[14]

Around the turn of the twentieth century, in the United States, there were a few alleged encounters with aliens. These landed in wooden or metal space ships that sported wings and propellers. One such account involved a farmer in Missouri who claimed he'd seen a vessel about twenty feet long and eight feet in diameter, with propellers about six feet across. Standing near the vessel, he claimed, was "the most beautiful thing I ever beheld. She was rather under medium size, but of the most exquisite form and features as would put to shame the forms as sculpted by the ancient Greeks. She was naked, dressed in nature's garb, and her golden hair, wavy and glossy, hung to her waist." Eventually, "some balls that were attached to the propellers began to revolve rapidly and the vessel took off as lightly as a bird and shot away like an arrow."[15]

In another account from the same year (1897), a West Virginia man walking home from a party looked up toward the night sky and saw an illuminated craft with propellers. It descended to the ground, and out stepped eight Martians, each eleven to twelve feet tall. They had come to explore Earth. They drank "air" and subsisted on small pills.[16]

In 1898, H. G. Wells published *The War of the Worlds*—a vivid and influential novel. A mysterious cylinder crashes to earth. Its top opens to release gray octopus-like creatures with tentacles and rimless lips that "drool saliva and quiver and pulsate." Wielding huge fighting machines, the creatures attack New York City with flaming gas. In 1938, Orson Welles and his Mercury Theatre broadcast a radio adaptation that became instantly famous. Many listeners who tuned in late thought they were listening to an actual news report instead of a radio play, and mass hysteria ensued. For weeks afterward, people kept telephoning police and fire departments to report seeing tentacled Martians poised for attack.[17]

George Adamski may have been the first commercially successful contactee. He owned a restaurant at the foot of Mount Palomar, in California, and the restaurant had a telescope out back. In 1953, he published a book about his encounter with aliens, but he did so under the name of "Professor Adamski" of the Mount Palomar Observatory. The book tells how, in a nearby desert, he came upon a group of nice-looking aliens; they had long blond hair and were dressed in white robes.[18] An interviewer at the time described him as a credible sort: "To listen to his story, you had an immediate urge to believe him. Maybe it was his appearance. He was dressed in well worn, but neat, overalls. He had slightly graying hair and the most honest pair of eyes I've ever seen."[19]

Despite these occasional otherworldly chats, no one appears to have been abducted by an alien until 1953, in the movie *Invaders from Mars*. In this film, big, green, humanoid aliens with oversized heads and eyes (they're nothing like the aliens that are fashionable today, but look more like robots) kidnap people from a small American town, anesthetize them with lights, and implant mind-control devices in the back of their necks. In one disturbing scene, a beautiful woman is placed on an operating table and a needle is stuck into her neck. In a later scene, a needle is inserted into her navel.

Two years later, another film depicted alien abduction. In *This Island Earth*, human scientists are kidnapped by aliens in flying saucers who need their help in order to save their planet. These aliens are also large-headed, robot-like humanoids, and the story features reversible amnesia.

The early 1960s brought more abductions, in a hugely popular TV series entitled *The Outer Limits*. A number of episodes in the years 1961–1964 explored the theme of abduction, and the aliens presented on this show looked a bit more similar to the ones reported today—more reptilian than robotic. One episode, "The Children of Spider County," featured aliens breeding with humans to create hybrids. Another episode, "Second Chance," showed big-headed, big-eyed aliens abducting humans for research purposes. In an episode called "Bellaro Shield," the aliens looked remarkably similar to those of today: they had big, black, wraparound eyes, no noses or mouths, and delicate waif-like bodies.[20]

At least twenty movies about extraterrestrials came out between 1951 *(The Day the Earth Stood Still)* and 1964, when the number of abduction reports began increasing. But only a handful of those films dealt with alien abduction. In most of them, aliens were coming to Earth to destroy us, or colonize us, or take over our bodies and minds. Humans were seldom abducted, but often went into space to fight with them on their own turf. In addition, those movie and TV aliens bore only a very general resemblance to today's iconic macrocephalic space-waifs. They were more likely to look like robots or reptiles, or a cross between the two. But whatever they looked like, they had disproportionately big heads, perhaps to suggest their technological sophistication. Who needs a body when you can control minds and harness other beings to do your work?

Recently a believer said to me, "If you're so sure that Hollywood influenced people's accounts, why is alien abduction the only thing that happens to us? There were a lot more movies that showed aliens taking over our bodies or attacking us. If your theory is correct, shouldn't we have come to believe that those things are happening to us as well?"

It's a good question, but I think it has a good answer. Abduction by aliens is the only one of the possible plots that cannot be objectively verified. If aliens were blowing up the Earth, you'd see it on the news. If they were taking over your body, scientists could perform physiological tests. In order to encounter them in space, you'd actually have to get there first. Alien abductions work really well because no one can say for sure that they didn't happen, and questions like "How did you float through the door?" or "Why didn't anyone else see the space ship?" can be answered with appeals to the aliens' technological superiority.

Now, it's true that flying saucers were first reported in 1947, before they were featured in movies or on television. But humans have been seeing machines in the sky—whether they were there or not—for a very long time.[21] During the 1890s, well before the Wright brothers' first flight at Kitty Hawk in 1903, there was a rumor that an American inventor had developed a "flying machine." The public promptly developed "airship mania," to the point that a journalist was able to joke, "The man who has not an airship in his backyard these days is poor indeed." Tens of thousands of people across the United States claimed to have seen the airship, with its cigar-shaped body, its propellers, and its bulky undercarriage.

The history of flying saucers began in Washington State, in June 1947. A businessman named Kenneth Arnold was piloting his private jet over the Cascade Mountains when he saw what appeared to be nine glittering objects, arranged like "geese in formation," moving rapidly through the sky. He kept them in sight for about three minutes. According to the transcript of the press conference, he said they were "crescent shaped" and "moved like a saucer would if you skipped it across the water." Though he never actually called them flying saucers, the media took the word "saucer" and played it up. The Associated Press story of the "flying saucers" ran in 150 newspapers. As Arnold put it himself in a 1950 interview, "The newspaper did not quote me properly. . . . When I told the press, they misquoted me, and in the excitement of it all, one newspaper and another got it so snarled up that nobody knew just exactly what they were talking about. . . . These objects more or less fluttered, like they were, oh, I'd say, boats on very rough water. . . . And when I described how they flew, I said that they flew like when you take a saucer and throw it across the water. Most of the newspapers misunderstood. . . . They said that I'd said they were saucer-like. I said they flew in a *saucer-like fashion*."[22]

Nonetheless, we've been seeing flying saucers ever since. After the story broke, people all across the country began spotting flying saucers. In 1951, posters for alien-invasion films started featuring them. The flying saucer is a social construction unique to the twentieth century. Yet just because people reported sightings didn't mean they thought flying saucers contained aliens. Only 5 percent of people who responded to a 1947 poll thought that saucers should be grouped with comets, stars, and other objects in outer space. Most believed that the United States Air Force or foreign military powers were responsible. Those were the early days of the Cold War, and Americans were far more afraid of terrestrial military invasions than extraterrestrial ones. As the *Chicago Sun* put it on July 8, 1947, a few weeks after Arnold's "saucers" were publicized:

"After a hard fourth of July weekend, the nation finds itself jittery over the subject of 'flying saucers.' Some people claim that they are jet-propelled and roar like night bombers. Others have them flying in formation, heading north. A gentleman in Denver says he saw the American flag painted on one of them. If this is true, this is certainly the most encouraging report to date. It will be merciful relief to many people who feared the disks might be of foreign origin. Human suggestibility being what it is, a lot of people didn't see what they say they saw."[23]

Ironically, this report came out on the very day that the so-called Roswell incident occurred. On June 14, near Roswell, New Mexico, a rancher had found some debris on the ground. He'd brought it into town on July 7. As was stated two days later in the

Roswell Daily Record, "The tinfoil, paper, tape, and sticks made a bundle about three feet long and seven or eight inches thick. Considerable scotch tape and some tape with flowers printed on it had been used in the construction." This pile of debris was linked to local sightings of a flying disc, which the U.S. military later identified as a radar-tracking balloon.[24]

The whole incident was forgotten for about three decades. Then, in February 1978, a former military officer named Jesse Marcel was quoted in the *National Enquirer* as saying that the debris constituted the remains of a wrecked spacecraft. In 1981 another tabloid, *The Globe,* ran a sensational story about a fellow named Oliver "Pappy" Henderson, who had found the cadavers of space aliens at the crash site and flown them to an air force base in Ohio. The escapade involving Henderson, who had since died, was reported by his elderly widow, Sappho.[25]

The real media frenzy began in 1980 with the publication of *The Roswell Incident,* co-written by one of the authors of *The Bermuda Triangle,* a blend of myth, hearsay, and folklore which had been published in 1974 and sold five million copies. Among the many bizarre claims made in *The Roswell Incident* was that pieces of aliens had been seen among the debris. This was attested to "by more than seventy witnesses who had some knowledge of the event."[26]

Despite the fact that the evidence for a crashed spaceship and dead extraterrestrials was entirely anecdotal, consisting of first-hand reports from people who "wished to remain anonymous" and even more tenuous second- and third-hand reports ("So-and-So told What's-His-Name, who told me that such-and-such really happened thirty years ago"), 65 percent of respondents to a 1997 poll said they thought that a spacecraft really had crashed in New

Mexico and that the government had engineered a cover-up. To this day, about 90,000 tourists a year trek to the dreary town of Roswell and pay good money to see the supposed crash site.[27]

What seems undeniable is that the sky is a vast screen on which we project our expectations and anxieties. When we expect flying machines, we see them. When we worry about invasion, we see foreign missiles. When—after a rash of publicity—we expect saucers, we see saucers.

By the mid-1950s, there were several popular books on the market saying that the flying saucers so many people were spotting might actually be extraterrestrial in nature. *The Flying Saucers Are Real,* by retired Major Donald Keyhoe, which sold half a million copies, argued that the U.S. government was covering up the truth about the reality of extraterrestrials.[28] Frank Scully's *Behind the Flying Saucers,* which sold 60,000 copies, claimed that extraterrestrials from crashed saucers were being kept in a secret military installation.[29] In *The Riddle of the Flying Saucers: Is Another World Watching?* science writer Gerald Heard also advocated an ET hypothesis.[30] Moreover, there were countless media reports of UFO sightings, big Hollywood movies about aliens, and a growing number of popular-magazine articles about aliens—all of which contributed to and reflected a growing social interest in the topic.

When did the American imagination begin putting all of this together into a single plot? When did people first "recover memories" of small gray beings with large black eyes and big heads who were abducting humans for medical and sexual experimentation?

It all seems to have started in 1964, during a series of hypnosis sessions involving a married couple, Betty and Barney Hill, and a Boston psychiatrist named Benjamin Simon. The alien-abduction experiences that the Hills recalled under hypnosis provided a template for all the abductions that followed. Theirs was the first abduction story of the modern genre. And they remembered it twelve days after ABC aired the "Bellero Shield" episode of *The Outer Limits.*[31]

Betty and Barney Hill were a middle-aged, interracial couple from New Hampshire. She was a social worker, and he had a job with the postal service. One night in 1961 they had been driving in the White Mountains. Betty had spotted a bright "star-like" object that seemed to be pursuing them. Nervous, they had turned off the main highway onto narrow mountain roads, arriving home two hours later than expected.

Soon after this experience, Betty had nightmares in which she and Barney were abducted and taken aboard the UFO. This is not so odd if you consider one important fact: Betty was a long-time believer. Or as Barney put it, "Yes, Betty did believe in flying saucers." He himself was not so certain. "I believe Betty is trying to make me think I saw a flying saucer." In addition, Betty was a fan of science fiction movies featuring aliens (she had seen *Invaders from Mars*) and had already read Donald Keyhoe's *Flying Saucers Are Real.* She wrote to Keyhoe at the research organization listed in the book, and soon received an answer: he suggested that her nightmares might have a basis in reality and that she ought to read Coral Lorazen's *Great Flying Saucer Hoax,* which included accounts of saucer-shaped UFOs that trailed cars along lonely country roads.

Within a year, Betty had started giving local talks about her UFO sighting and her bad dreams. Sometime around 1963 she and Barney were advised to undergo hypnosis, in order to determine whether, as she firmly suspected, they had been abducted. Keep in mind that a number of popular movies (such as *Killers from Space;* 1954) had already used the motif of reversible amnesia.

In 1964, in the course of four months of hypnotherapy, the

couple separately filled in details of what had happened during what they now believed were their "missing" two hours. It took a number of sessions for a coherent narrative to emerge. They had watched the UFO land on the highway, and had been taken, partly immobilized, inside the spacecraft. Gray humanoid creatures with big eyes had subjected them to unconventional medical examinations, which had included the insertion of a needle into Betty's navel. Remember that Betty had seen *Invaders from Mars,* in which the aliens were gray humanoids with big eyes, a female abductee was poked and prodded by the creatures, and needles were inserted into her neck and navel.

Betty and Barney's experiences were shared with the world in *The Interrupted Journey,* by John Fuller, a bestseller published in 1966. But their story as presented in the book bears only a faint resemblance to the version recorded in the transcripts of their hypnosis sessions—also included in Fuller's book.

Here is how the event was initially described by Barney under hypnosis:[32]

"I was sitting out there on that mountain road at night. I could actually see what I described as the Cheshire cat. This glowing, one-beam eye staring at me—or rather, not staring at me but right through me. . . . One alien person looks friendly to me; he's friendly-looking. And he's looking at me over his right shoulder, and he's smiling."

"What does the face make you think of?" asks the hypnotist.

"It was round. I think of . . . a red-headed Irishman," says Barney.

But later on in the session, the alien has an "evil face. . . . He looks like a German Nazi. He has a black scarf around his neck, dangling over his right shoulder . . . Oh! I feel like a rabbit!"

"Why do you feel like a rabbit?" Dr. Simon asks.

"I was hunting for rabbits in Virginia. And this cute little bunny went into a bush that was not very big. . . . And the poor little bunny thought he was safe. . . . He was just hiding behind a little stalk which meant security to him, when I pounced on him, and captured the poor little bunny who thought he was safe. Funny I thought of that. Right there out in the field. I felt like a rabbit."

In another regression session Barney tried to describe the alien "leader," who was wearing a "black shiny jacket and scarf. I've never seen eyes slanted like that. His eyes were slanted. Oh, his eyes were slanted—but not like a Chinese! They began round and went back like that, and like that, and they went up like this. . . . Please, can I draw it?"

"Yes, you can draw whatever you want," said the therapist—and the picture that Barney drew made alien-icon history. It was featured in the book, was used by special-effects artists for the 1975 TV movie about the couple's experience, and then was recycled by Steven Spielberg in his 1977 film *Close Encounters of the Third Kind.*

The problem is that, contrary to what Barney said, he *had* seen eyes like that. "The Bellero Shield," which had aired twelve days before his regression session, featured the same eyes.

Now here's Barney description of the aliens in John Fuller's book: "The men had rather odd-shaped heads, with a large cranium, diminishing in size as it got toward the chin. And the eyes continued around to the sides of their heads, so that it appeared that they could see several degrees beyond the lateral extent of our vision. . . . I didn't notice any hair—or headgear, for that matter. Also, I didn't notice any proboscis. There just seemed to be two slits that represented the nostrils. So it looked as if the mouth had almost no opening and as if they had no nose."

Here's a passage typical of what Betty Hill remembered under hypnosis: "Oh—and then they take off my shoes and they look at my feet. And they look at my hands—they examine my hands all over. . . . And he takes something and he goes underneath my fingernail and then he—I don't know, probably manicure scissors or something—and he cuts off a piece of my fingernail. . . . Then the doctor, the examiner, says he wants to do some tests; he wants to check my nervous system. And I am thinking, 'I don't know how our nervous systems are, but I hope we never have nerve enough to go around kidnapping people right off the highways, as he has done!' And, oh, he tells me to take off my dress, and then, before I even have a chance hardly to stand up to do it, the examiner . . ."

Betty is interrupted by the hypnotist: "Does your dress have a zipper down the back?" Yes, it does.

"He unzips it, and so I slip my dress off. . . . I lie down on the table, on my back, and he brings over this—oh, how can I describe it? They're like needles, a whole cluster of needles, and each needle has a wire going from it, to, uh . . . I think it's something like a TV screen. You know—when the picture isn't on and you get all kinds of lines. . . . He rolls me over on my back, and the examiner has a long needle in his hand. . . . It's bigger than any needle that I've ever seen. . . . He says he just wants to put it in my navel; it's just a simple test. . . . No, it will hurt! Don't do it, don't do it! . . . It's hurting, it's hurting! Take it out, take it out! . . . I don't know why they put that needle into my navel. Because I told them they shouldn't do it. . . . Why did they put that needle in my navel? And he said it was a pregnancy test."

The abduction of Betty and Barney Hill became a media sensation. It was described in Fuller's popular book and in a made-for-TV movie starring Estelle Parsons and James Earl Jones. The movie was meretriciously presented as a sort of documentary, and its impact was immediate. "A rash of abduction reports followed in the wake of the NBC movie. A UFO organization compiled statistics showing that from 1947 to 1976 there were only fifty abduction reports, total [an average of two per year]. But in the two years following the broadcast, there were over a hundred cases—a 2,500 percent increase." The conclusion of the skeptic who wrote this passage? "After viewing this movie, any person with a little imagination could now become an instant celebrity."[33]

One of those instant celebrities was Travis Walton. He was abducted two weeks after the movie aired, and he described the experience on national TV. It was quite similar to the Betty and Barney's abduction, except for a few details. His "grays" were wearing orange overalls, and he also saw a beautiful alien couple with blond hair. He turned his account into a popular book called *The Walton Experience* (1978), which was made into a movie (1993), and then he spun it into another book called *Fire in the Sky* (1996).[34]

The small gray alien with big wraparound eyes was quickly recycled for *The Andreasson Affair* (1979), a book about the abduction experience of a Massachusetts woman named Betty Andreasson. The author, Raymond Fowler, a hypnotist, freely acknowledged that what Andreasson recalled under hypnosis was remarkably similar to the "UFO abduction case involving Betty and Barney Hill that was described in John Fuller's *The Interrupted Journey*."[35]

An excerpt from the Andreasson transcripts:

"And now they are going over there and talking. Oh boy, I'll be glad when this is all over with! Now they are looking at me. They are coming over again. And they are saying they have to measure me for procreation. . . . They are getting ready to do something.

. . . They are down by my feet somewhere. They are doing something there. They are not touching me, but they are doing something. It must be something down there they are preparing. Now they are pulling something. That needle again, with a tube, like, on the end. They are pulling—it looks like he's going to put it in me. Oh! And he's opening up my shirt, and—he's going to put that thing in my navel. Ohhhh, I don't like this! . . . I can feel them moving that thing around in my stomach, in my body. . . . Oh! He's pushing that around again, feeling things. I don't like this! Feeling like he is going right through my stuff inside. . . . Ohhhhh boy! He's stopped again. . . . Ahhh . . . He's starting to take the thing out. Ohhhhh. Ahhhhh. Thank you."

At another point, "They took those long silver needles—they were bendable—and they stuck one up my nose and into my head. . . . They said they were awakening something. When they stuck that needle up my nose, I heard something break, like a membrane or a veil or something, like a piece of tissue or something they broke through."[36]

This passage sounded awfully familiar to me. And it'll sound familiar to you, too: it's remarkably similar to a case in John Mack's *Abduction*—a transcript that I quoted from in Chapter 3: "He was looking at my nostril, and he put it in as far as it could go. I didn't like it, because I couldn't breathe very well. And then he hit something in the back and he just kind of pushed it, and he pushed it through whatever it was. [*Now sobbing*] I could feel something breaking in my head. . . . I'm wondering what they broke."[37] Obviously, John Mack's subject had read or heard about Andreasson's experience.

Probably the most famous abductee was Whitley Strieber. His 1987 book *Communion* became a *New York Times* bestseller—the first book on alien abduction to achieve such a distinction. The graphic content (a female alien wants to have sex with him, but he has difficulty getting an erection) may have had something to do with its success. Strieber describes one of his visitors as looking "not quite as naked as the creature that emerged in the movie *Close Encounters of the Third Kind.*" He not only admits to having seen many films about aliens prior to his own encounter; he also says he's "read thousands of pages of material about the whole ET and UFO phenomenon."

When his hypnotist asks him to describe the female alien, "to look very hard at it," Strieber replies: "She's staring right back at me. She looks like a big bug. Really big, black eyes. . . . She's thin. . . . The eyes are slanted more than an Oriental's eyes."

The hypnotist then asks, "Have you ever seen an image like this?" Whitley says no, despite having mentioned "reading something in *Look* magazine about the Betty and Barney Hill abduction."

The hypnotist presses him. "Are you *sure* you haven't seen an image like this? What about the book you have?"

And Strieber replies tellingly, "In our culture there's just so much media around. It's possible, but I don't think so, because this is so damn real. . . . It seems impossible that it could be an image I picked up from somewhere."[38]

But Strieber was on to something. Abduction reports were being published at an ever-increasing rate. They seemed to feed on one another. Each new account absorbed details from previous accounts, leading to the "consistency" that so intrigues believers. Betty and Barney Hill got their ideas from books, movies, and TV. From then on, people got their ideas from books, movies, TV, and Betty and Barney Hill—and whoever the next media-star abductee happened to be.

Today, "there's just so much media around" that we all know

what aliens look like and what they do. If you don't believe me, draw one. See? Now imagine being abducted. I can pretty much guarantee that under hypnosis you'd come out with the standard story—though afterward, of course, you probably wouldn't believe it was true. It would be embellished with your own details (what the aliens wore, what the purpose of the abduction was, why you were chosen, what specifically was done to you and how), but the *general plot* would be the same as in all the other accounts: "I was abducted by grayish aliens with big heads and big eyes who did things to my body."

Research substantiating this was done a long time ago. In 1978 scientists recruited volunteers claiming to have little interest in extraterrestrial life, and hypnotized them. They then told the subjects to imagine an alien encounter in which they saw a UFO, were taken aboard the craft, were given a physical exam, and so on. The data indicated that the hypnotically suggested reports were not much different from "real" reports by abductees.[39] It seems that after a surprisingly short time—only two years after Betty and Barney's story was presented on TV, only one year after Travis Walton's book was published, and only one year after Spielberg's *Close Encounters of the Third Kind* was released—elements of the alien-contact narrative were circulating widely among the general public.

In 1994, Steven Jay Lynn extended Lawson's findings. He didn't even have to hypnotize people to extract a UFO encounter—he just had them simulate hypnotized people. But in response to hypnotists' suggestions, his role-playing subjects still reported UFO encounters involving gray aliens, medical experiments, and UFOs. Obviously, elements of the UFO script are part of our popular culture.

I tried something similar with my graduate students in Nicaragua: I asked them to draw pictures of space aliens. Nicaragua is a long way from Hollywood and from Betty and Barney Hill's New Hampshire. It's what the U.S. government calls a "hyper-indebted poor country." Nevertheless, my students drew macrocephalic gray waifs with wraparound eyes, and told me what these aliens did: they abducted you in order to experiment on you and "make babies with you."

Of course, those young Nicaraguans were well educated and generally attuned to Western cultural references. If I've focused on the United States in this book, it's because the abduction scenario hardly exists cross-culturally.[40] People in Brazil or Kenya or Vietnam may see weird things in the sky, but rarely anything that comes down and kidnaps them for medical or sexual purposes. John Mack himself noted that UFO abduction reports are more frequent in "Western countries or countries dominated by Western cultural values."[41] This could change, though, as movies and TV shows like *The X-Files* get exported more widely. In May 2005 an Agence France-Presse correspondent based in Beijing noted that Chinese people have been reporting more alien encounters, perhaps because they have "lost their spiritual bearings" as Marxism has given way to materialism.[42]

Certainly in the United States the image of the typical extraterrestrial is fixed in people's minds almost from the cradle. At the tender age of two and a half, my daughter knew what aliens looked like. I once watched a TV show with her—a kids' program about a little boy who would eat carrots, and then the things he imagined would become real (or something like that). In the episode we saw, he imagined going into space and meeting aliens. They looked just like aliens do, though more brightly colored. Later, I turned on *South Park*—an episode in which one of the characters was abducted. When my little girl saw the extraterrestrials, she pointed excitedly: "Look, Mommy, aliens!" A toddler who couldn't reliably tell the difference between a cat and a dog could identify an alien instantly. Clearly, she'd already watched too much TV.

After two years of intense alienography, this is what I conclude. Aliens are entirely and extremely human, the imaginative creations of people with ordinary emotional needs and desires. We don't want to be alone. We feel helpless and vulnerable much of the time. We want to believe there's something bigger and better than us out there. And we want to believe that whatever it is cares about us, or at least is paying attention to us. That they want us (sexually or otherwise). That we're special. Being abducted by aliens is a culturally shaped manifestation of a universal human need.

As Carl Jung put it in *Flying Saucers: The Myth of Things Seen in the Sky,* "The unconscious has to resort to particularly drastic measures in order to make its content perceived. It does this most vividly by projection, by extrapolating its content into an object, which then mirrors what had previously lay hidden in the unconscious. . . . They [flying saucers] are based essentially on an omnipresent emotional foundation, in this case a psychological situation common to all mankind."[43]

Jung has a point. Yet at the same time, doesn't the alien-abduction experience portray a rather banal universe? If somehow the incredible odds against the evolution of intelligent life have been overcome elsewhere in the cosmos, and those aliens are so advanced that they can build technologically unimaginable spacecraft and travel light years with ease, why would they come visit *us?* And why, having done so, would they be interested in manually harvesting eggs and sperm with shiny metal devices on operating tables? Today is but a fleeting moment in the history of our species, and our history as a species is but a fleeting moment in the context of the universe. Wouldn't you think these mentally and technologically superior beings would have something more interesting to do (something quite possibly beyond the imagining of the human brain) than to hang around North America kidnapping its more creative and intuitive inhabitants, in order to do the same experiments over and over again? Why are these genius aliens so dim? After fifty years of abducting us, why are they are still taking the same bits and pieces? Don't they have freezers?

Not a single alien I have ever heard described is as fascinating and surprising as the average human child. The common features of the alien-abduction stories—the elements of the basic plot—are not evidence of validity. They are evidence that these stories have been contrived out of shared cultural knowledge and shared psychological fears, needs, hopes, and limitations.

Truly, the only interesting thing about alien-abduction narratives is the fact that they vary so idiosyncratically from person to person. I love to hear all the vivid, inventive details—the differences in clothing (track suits, orange overalls, flowing white robes, nothing except for cherry-red pubic hair), the various styles of conversation (rude, kind, regal, telepathic, none at all), the ways they take off your clothes ("They ripped them off like a bunch of horny teenagers. . . . By the time I was on the ship, I was wearing only my cowboy boots and my husband's white T-shirt"), the particular method they use to extract your semen or your eggs (magnetic devices, suction tubes, long shiny pincers, ice-cream-cone-shaped tools where the ice-cream part was rotating really fast). As Carl Jung is reputed to have said, "When facts are few, speculations are most likely to represent individual psychology."

5 Who Gets Abducted?

M_y alien-abduction research provokes lots of questions. Most of these focus not on the abduction experiences themselves, but on the people who have them. Are they nuts? Attention-crazed? Sexually deviant? Do they *look* normal?

There's a voyeuristic aspect to these questions. Beneath much of the interest is the implicit assumption that the abductees are excitingly weird.

So, are they? It depends. If I compare them to the well-educated readers of university press books like this one, then the abductees are about 1.5 standard deviations from the norm, on a continuum I'll tentatively label "weirdness." But if I compare them to other groups I've had close contact with—serious vegetarians, yoga enthusiasts, artists, Hollywood actors, psychologists, Internet entrepreneurs, or my family—they really don't look all that different.

I liked them. I didn't like listening to the sexual-experimentation stories. I didn't like hearing the more extreme and bizarre abduction details (the anal probe that fell out, was analyzed by a lab, and declared to be a hemorrhoid because "they were afraid of the truth"). And I was dismayed by the abductees' collective lack of skepticism and scientific thinking. But apart from that, I enjoyed my time with these research subjects far more than the time I spent interviewing other groups—depressives, hypochondriacs, patients suffering from post-traumatic stress, alcoholics, healthy Harvard undergraduates, assistant professors. They were generally warm, open, trusting, and friendly. After social gatherings, they'd send photos. After interviews, they'd send thank-you notes. I still receive Christmas cards from some of them.

Yes, there were a few I didn't like—paranoid, angry, hostile, and quasi-psychotic. But these were few and far between. Of the approximately fifty abductees I interviewed, there were only three I had problems relating to.

One was Bill. Bill was forty-five, on his third marriage, and self-employed as an "intuitive"—meaning that "people and sometimes companies hire me to give them advice based on my intuitive abilities." He was a big, bearish fellow, and was missing an arm as the result of a childhood accident. When he was twelve, he'd received an electric shock from a power line and had developed gangrene (an event he had since come to attribute to aliens). Though he was married, he had multiple sex partners. One of them had once revealed herself, in mid-act, to be an alien. I have a vivid memory of Bill sitting in my office, describing his sexual encounter with the woman, telling me how she suddenly "switched" into her alien self and he "tossed her off" his lap and ran out the door.

Another difficult subject was Athena—a forty-seven-year-old

single woman. She was tall and striking, with long wavy black hair and an olive complexion, and she wore many layers of synthetic black and purple material that swished around her when she moved. Athena was a professional "channeler," mostly for alien spirits. Our interview took place on a dark snowy Saturday, in late afternoon. The lab was deserted. At her request I left the door open, and I could hear our voices echoing weirdly down the empty hallway.

Athena asked if she could light a candle, to "relax" her, and halfway through the interview she got spacey. It took longer and longer for her to answer questions, and her answers were increasingly tangential. "How old where you when you had your first memory of being abducted by aliens?" She stared into space for about ten seconds, and then replied: "I remember I was an odd child, prone to spending time alone in the woods. I could commune better with the creatures of the forest than with my own family." Eventually, she stopped answering questions altogether and closed her eyes. Then the upper half of her body began to tremble and she fell to her knees, staring upward, spine rigid. Before I could call Security, she began speaking in a new voice—low and feathery. She'd been contacted by an alien who wanted to tell me something. Was this okay?

What could I say? "No, you're too weird"? This was, after all, a research project, and I felt grimly that I had a scientific obligation to listen to whatever she wanted to share with me. For the next thirty-three minutes, all caught on tape, Athena channeled a female alien—a member of an elite sisterhood located living on the planet Astralia, in a distant solar system. Among the revelations that emerged during the session: I was doing this research because I was part alien myself. My first abduction had come in 1996, and I'd given birth to a hybrid baby. My child was "up there and aware of my loving presence."

When Athena asked if I wanted to communicate with my alien offspring, I told her I'd been channeled enough. I couldn't take the weirdness anymore, and was flushed and sweaty. I could handle bizarre behavior in the context of diagnosable psychopathology (I'd once had a schizophrenic try to gnaw his arm off during an interview), but not from subjects who came to me as ostensibly normal people.

Athena was really nice about the whole thing. She told me my discomfort was quite natural, considering what I'd just learned about my alien heritage. Since she channeled all sorts of people in every region of the country, she was, she assured me, quite used to this type of reaction.

The third subject I had trouble with was Steven—a heroin addict and Vietnam vet. He was a nice guy, but largely incoherent, highly influenced by 1970s music, and prone to steeping himself in patchouli before our interviews. I don't remember why anyone thought that chauffeuring him around was a good idea, but I used to drive him from his halfway house in Boston to the lab in New Hampshire. On the way, we would stop at a Dunkin Donuts he liked. I distinctly remember the two of us cruising down the Mass Pike, listening to Three Dog Night and balancing black coffee and sugar donuts on our laps, while he pointed out a UFO in the sky that he suspected was following him (it was a traffic helicopter). His scent lingered in my car for a long time and was one of the primary reasons I sold it later that year.

None of these three subjects finished the research protocol. But they did at least make it through the interview stage. Many people never got past the screening call. Some of them were mentally ill. They were easy to identify because they either thought they were ETs ("I'm an alien—help me!") or because they were currently in the proximity of UFOs ("It's parked in my basement") or extraterrestrials ("They're here, right now, communicating with me—and they want me to stop you").

As for the rest of the subjects, all those kind and generous people who gave me their time and shared their beliefs and experiences, I'll let you meet them in the same order I did. I'll allow you a brief peek into their appearance, personality, and "clinical presentation" (though of course names and identifying details have been changed). The advantage of doing this is that you can get a sense of them as I did, before I became inured to their stories and before many of them had dropped out of the study.

At the beginning of my research, I probably had a more representative cross-section of believers. They came from all socioeconomic strata and were quite varied in ethnicity, age, and strength of attachment to their beliefs. These are the folks you'll meet below. But over time, the group became more homogeneous. The word got out, and I developed a reputation in the Boston community. Many abductees shied away from the research because they feared it would further tarnish their credibility. The ones that didn't avoid me tended to be more established in the "abduction community," more confident in their beliefs and memories, more personally invested in their abduction experiences, more likely to have sought help in eliciting their memories in the first place, and more likely to have networked with other abductees. You can read about such people in the work of other abduction researchers

(John Mack, Budd Hopkins, David Jacobs, John Fuller). The sort of individual I introduce here generally doesn't appear elsewhere.

One of my first subjects was Tom, a freckled twenty-two-year-old from New Hampshire—a really nice kid. He was single, a high school graduate, worked in construction, and lived with his parents in a room he'd built under their house (one of his first construction jobs). Tom didn't have any abduction memories yet, but strongly suspected that he would soon. "I believe in aliens. I'm an armchair kind of scientist." He called to participate in the study because "about a month ago I got out of the shower and looked at my back and saw bruises. I thought maybe I'd slept on coins. They were a donut shape with skin color in the middle. I thought it was pretty weird, but I didn't jump to any conclusions. Then I talked to my Mom about it, and she looked at my back and said, 'Well, maybe aliens' . . . I still thought coins, but the marks weren't reddish. They were, like, kind of black or purplish."

Tom asked for a second opinion from his best friend. "He said it *could* be aliens, but he also said that since I'm working on a demolition job, maybe it's that." Despite this very reasonable interpretation of the marks, Tom was still "pretty sure it was aliens. I have a strong feeling about it. I try my best to be open-minded. It's how I go through life."

Tom had the marks on his back photographed. He gave the pictures to me, just in case I wanted to "send them out for analysis."

Tom and his parents were very interested in alien phenomenology; they'd read a number of books and seen many movies about aliens. "I really liked that book *Communion,* by Whitley Strieber. It was *awesome*. Also, I'm on the Internet all the time researching aliens. There's a lot of amazing stuff out there."

Not only was Tom sure that something had happened, but he'd read that "the only way to get memories of what happened is by using hypnotherapy. Do you know anyone I could call about that?"

The same week I met Tom, I interviewed Mudar. He was from Palestine but had been in the United States for three years. He was very vague about what he did for a living and why he lived in the boonies of New England. What I do know is that he was twenty-eight and unmarried, had an MBA from the University of New Hampshire, and lived in an apartment complex with four friends from his homeland. He stated adamantly that, as a Muslim, he did not drink, smoke, or use drugs. He was short, dark, and handsome, and he dressed all in black—black jeans, black turtle-neck, slipper-like black loafers. He was conspicuously out of place in New Hampshire, amid all the plaid shirts and work boots.

Mudar had been abducted two years previously, after an evening out with some friends. He'd come home and fallen asleep with his clothes on, but woke up without them. "Aliens were looking at me. I was naked, not 100 percent naked but 90 percent naked. I had a cloth on my genitals."

Mudar believed that the creatures were extraterrestrials. His family supported him in his belief, as did his faith. According to the Muslim religion, he said, God created two kinds of creatures: humans and the "others." "They have the ability to take different forms and shapes."

Unlike other abductees, Mudar did not report feeling terror. "I did not feel afraid. In my mind, the sense of it was that this was a regular experience for me. Like, in some other dimension this happens regularly, and for some reason I was just made aware of it that night." Later in the interview, he explicitly said that his experiences were consistent with his religious views. God created another species, represented by the aliens, and so it shouldn't be surprising that we have contact with them. He repeatedly suggested that I read the Koran, where I could find "proof" of alien beings. "The Koran talks about how people can be occupied by aliens. They can live in them. In my country, people are being occupied by these creatures. In your country, I saw a documentary on demonic possession. They are not demons—they are aliens. There is a consistent pattern."

As a routine part of the interview, subjects were asked if they believed in astrology. Mudar gave a very firm answer: "No. Astrology is not logical."

A few weeks later I interviewed Debra. She was forty-one, fair-skinned and blond, attractive and overweight. She had a high school equivalency degree, and was supporting herself by working the counter at a sandwich shop and cleaning houses on the side. Twice married, she had a seventeen-year-old son. Though she came to my office on a cold winter day, she was wearing a Hawaiian shirt. Right up front, she wanted me to know that "all my life I've felt like an outcast. Like I'm different from others, but not in a good way. I just want to feel normal when I wake up. All my life I've been fighting against self-destruction. I've been an alcoholic, a compulsive eater, addicted to pain killers—you name it and I've probably abused it."

Debra had had her first experience when her son, Bob, was three. She'd been lying on the couch, facing the wall, listening to David Letterman on TV, "when I heard a really loud noise, an unbearable noise, and the whole sky lit up." At that point, she'd realized she was paralyzed and couldn't get up. "Then I was lifted off the ground and floated somewhere. I remember being in a room. There were people on tables. Things looking at them. I thought I was going to die with fear. They weren't mean—just kind of like doing their job. I remember a tall being coming out and telling me that things were going to be okay, and I felt better. He had compassion. Then I remember waking up, and my son was on the floor next to me and he was crying."

Although this was her only memory of abduction, she was sure she was being "taken" fairly regularly. She based this belief on the fact that she would wake up "in weird positions," that her son had heard her "struggling one night with her bedclothes," that she would "wake up sweaty," and that her memory was bad. "When they take you, they have to wipe out your memories. But they aren't perfect, and they can wipe out other normal memories with the abduction ones."

Debra believed that the purpose of her abduction was "for creating hybrid babies." This made her sad. "I feel like there's a piece of me missing. I have a sense of loss. I think there's a little girl up there who is part mine, an alien girl with blond wispy hair. Like a cancer victim. But she doesn't want any part of me—she would rather stay up there."

Bob had also had experiences. He was tall and skinny, and wore his dark brown hair spiky on top. After graduating from high school, he said, he wanted to enroll at the CIA—not the Central Intelligence Agency, but the Culinary Institute of America. He'd always loved cooking. Bob said, "When I'm not worrying, I sleep normally. But when I'm worried about something, then it happens. I'll be lying there. Then I'll hear a noise like a helicopter. I see a white light. Then I can't move. There are hands reaching out, touching me. Then I'm put back in another holding position. When I wake up, I know I've been abducted because I'm sleeping in another position. Usually I sleep vertically."

Bob said he remembered the night his mom was first abducted—when he was three. "I remember I was going to the bathroom. Then I remember going out the window and feeling like I was moving up and down. I remember seeing them. Long and tall. Big black eyes. Gray. No hair, no nose. I remember talking to them, but not talking—telepathically, like they were telling me their experiences in my mind. I remember seeing other kids there. There was a little red-haired boy. I remembered I wanted to be able to play with him."

Bob didn't know why he got abducted, but, like his mother, he believed it happened a lot. "I know it happens because I get nosebleeds. My dad thinks it's a transmitter they put in there."

He also wondered if perhaps he was part alien. "I'm a little darker than my mom and dad. I wonder if they harvested eggs?"

Bob's girlfriend came to the interview. She was pale, overweight, dressed entirely in black, and wearing two nose rings. She believed his accounts. She had helped him to notice scratches and strange marks on his body, and they both linked these to abduction experiences.

Although the father did not report being abducted himself, he was a believer. Both mother and son reported that "he wants it to happen to him." Bob told me: "He has about fifty UFO movies, and he makes me watch them with him. In 1998 he went to that

Roswell place, and he thinks while he was there he might have seen a UFO."

"I've dealt with this my whole life," Bob said. "I don't think they're going to stop, and I don't care. Because I don't think they want to hurt me. I hope they take my dad too. And if they do, I hope they take him with my mother because I wouldn't want him to be afraid."

A few weeks later, I interviewed Dr. James Anderson, a fifty-year-old dermatologist at a Harvard-affiliated Boston hospital. He was tall and fit, and was wearing a crisp blue-striped Brooks Brothers shirt, khakis, and nice shoes. He was happily married and had three kids. He referred to himself as "a skeptical vegetarian" and "an occasional Christian." When asked a routine question about past medical or psychological problems, he said he hadn't had any—"but if anything is going to drive me crazy, it's my daughter going through puberty."

James had had an experience in 1973, when he was a student at the University of Southern California in Los Angeles. He'd been driving north with some friends on a ski trip. "There were three of us in the car. We were on a two-lane road going through the Mojave desert. It was nighttime. I saw a huge cylindrical object—saucer shaped, wide in the middle with lights, size of a football field—hovering about a hundred feet off the ground. Or perhaps it was much further up and was just enormous. I didn't know. I felt terror. It was about nine P.M., a very dark night in January. I woke up my friend Mike in the back seat. He saw it too, and wanted to drive closer. I've never felt terror like that, before or since. It was hovering above us. I put my foot on the pedal. Time elapsed. The terror abated. Once I'd taken action, I felt peaceful and calm. I lost time that night—I don't know what happened for a few hours after I saw it."

Today, he's quite confident that he and his friends were abducted that night, that the aliens erased his memories, and that he will never get those memories back.

I inquired about the friend who had been awake with him. Did the friend think he'd been abducted too? "No, I don't think so. We didn't really want to talk about it afterward. Just a huge reluctance to talk about it, like we just didn't want to focus on it. . . . I've lost touch with him. . . . We just never talked about it afterward.

"I was always interested in space travel. Afterward I sort of had this anger against the aliens. It makes me very angry that they could just do that to us. What truly makes me believe is the time lapse—that's the thing that convinced me. I think it's interesting that three hours passed and I don't know what happened. I didn't really focus on that part much, until I read something about it. I think it was Whitley Strieber's book *Communion*."

I asked James whether he thought the book had influenced his beliefs. "Well, I've been very careful not to let what I've read become part of what I think happened. I think hypnosis can cause you to implant false memories. That's why I'm not going that route."

I asked how his family had reacted to his account. "My wife says she believes I saw something, but thinks it must have been something 'logical.' And my twelve-year-old daughter is terrified of aliens. She can't watch movies or TV shows about alien stuff. . . . The whole subject bothers her. . . . I hope they haven't had contact with her.

"I have a love/hate relationship with the whole alien thing. I'm drawn to it, but then it really frightens me. It makes me angry. Who do they think they are that they can just do this to us, as if we're nothing to them?"

That same week, I interviewed Steve, a forty-five-year-old single librarian. He was irritable, nerdy, and neat. Before I could even ask him about his background, he informed me that (1) abductions are similar to near-death experiences, but at the end of the tunnel of light you see an alien instead of God; (2) he very much admired NASA's Search for Extraterrestrial Intelligence (SETI) program; and (3) nonbelievers laugh off abduction claims in two ways: they ascribe them to false memories or to sleep paralysis. He wanted to know if I thought either explanation was valid. I gave my routine answer: that I was doing my best to collect data from experiencers in order to shed more light on the phenomenon.

Steve told me that he'd been seeing a psychologist since he was six. "People say I was quite atypical as a child. I was adopted at an early age. Maybe I was from a test tube. I often wonder if I really belong in outer space. . . . I was always interested in science fiction. I always wanted to see a UFO. Even at eleven I remember looking at meteor showers, hoping to see something. Then, when I was twenty-one, I drove from California to New Mexico. I was traveling in a rickety truck. I saw a light, then saw many lights. They shone down on me from above the truck, but they were spread out. They kept flashing—on the left side, in the middle, on the right side. This went on for maybe twenty or thirty seconds. I was so scared! I didn't know what to do, but I kept driving. . . . You know, the lights I saw were a lot like the ones in the movie *Close Encounters*.

"I've read Whitley Strieber's *Communion*. It really creeps me out—but, still, it intrigues me. Why is this? You know, when I was in my thirties I quit smoking and gained a lot of weight. I went to a hypnotist for help, to try to stop smoking. I only went to one session. I don't know exactly what happened, but I started having this flood of memories, this explosion related to what I saw that night. The memories were coming back. I know something happened. I know I was abducted. I know something was there." He firmly believed he could access his abduction experience through hypnosis—if he wanted to. "I'm just not sure I'm ready to know."

Later in the interview he said, "If I was abducted, it explains a lot. Why I've never fit in. Why I've always been interested in science fiction and metaphysics. You know, they say that UFOs are the religion of the scientific. There's a lot of truth in that. I'm very attracted to mysticism and aliens are a shortcut. Raymond Fowler's book *The Watchers* was great. He really gets me. The idea that they could be the watchers, the aliens: the gods."

I heard from Steve fairly regularly via email after our interview. He used to send me alien-related material from the Internet—information that he felt would be useful to my research. And three times he sent me clippings from printed articles about UFO sightings and reported abductions—complete with his long commentaries scrawled in the margins.

Jan was the next subject I spoke with. She was a tall, willowy fifty-eight-year-old dressed in jeans, a red turtleneck, and a green vest. A divorcee with children, she now identified herself as a lesbian and was living with her partner in a wealthy suburb of Boston. She was employed as a spa-cuisine chef at a well-known resort.

In 1988 she'd been vacationing in Guana, India. She and four people had been sitting on the beach in the early evening when they'd spotted a silver object in the sky above them, moving very fast. "I was *not* on any drugs or alcohol. . . . It was the most amazing thing I've ever seen. . . . If you looked away, you couldn't find it—you had to look *into* space. It was the most amazing thing! . . . Space itself appeared multidimensional. Then the object came closer, as close as the low-lying clouds. One person we were with—she channeled it. . . . It spoke to us."

I asked for details about the channeling. It turned out that the person was "a high spirit. She's more connected to the other world than anyone I ever met. There's another world out there, and she is part of it. Because she's a high spirit, she could address it in a humble way. It communicated with us for fifteen minutes or so. It spoke to *her*, actually, but it said it acknowledged her friends. It said that it had come here to watch over us, to observe, and that it wasn't going to return. But later on that night, when we were walking to a restaurant I saw the light again, and it was coming closer. I said, 'It's here!' but she didn't say anything—she just acknowledged it. Then it took off, disappeared."

This enigmatic event had had a huge impact on Jan. "After that experience in India, I knew I had to follow that woman, to be near her and to learn from her. So I moved with her to Hong Kong. . . . She taught me so much. She's a Taoist priestess; she has had temple training. She taught me to be macrobiotic, to celebrate my body with dance and yoga. She showed me how she channels spirits . . . and with her help I learned that that wasn't the first time I'd seen aliens. When I was sixteen, at Nantasket Beach—it was night and I was alone, and I saw a light that circled around me and then was gone. Now I know it was a UFO."

At a later point in the interview, she discussed the aliens themselves. "You know, they do walk among us on the earth. They have to transform first into a physical body, which is very painful for them, and they do it out of love. They are here to tell us that everything we do affects everything else, that we're all interconnected in some way. Everything is. And they protect us so we can't be destructive to ourselves." I asked how she knew this. "It's what I know. It just is. That's all. You can't ask them questions like, 'What are you? Why are you here? How have you intervened on our behalf?' You just need to know."

Not surprisingly, Jan endorsed a number of "alternative" beliefs. She was an avid practitioner of yoga and meditation. She believed in herbal medicine, so wholeheartedly that she never went to physicians. She was an advocate of Chinese astrology and macrobiotic nutrition. My experience with macrobiotic food is that it's brown and it tastes bad, so I asked why she liked it.

"Well, ten years ago I was on this health-food diet of only uncooked food, but I was hungry all the time. Then I went to a friend's house for lunch and she gave me brown rice and miso soup and I was like, 'Oh my God—this is the food for me!' She told me about macrobiotic diet and its importance. I attended a macro camp in the Poconos for a month. I changed my diet, changed my life. I got rid of my belongings—except for my piano, car, and clothes—and moved closer to a macro community in Boston. The first night in my new home I went to Open Sesame, this macro restaurant in Newton. In it were these three beautiful women, wearing the most beautiful, flowing, elegant clothes. These were just the most elegant women in the world. I've been macro since then."

*   *   *

Next was Sam: sixty-five, twice divorced, currently single. He referred to himself as "unlucky in love." A community-college graduate, he worked as a maintenance supervisor for a construction firm. He looked reassuringly like my grandfather, but what emerged during the interview was not so grandfatherly.

"In 1991 my wife, Patty, and I went to a health exposition in the city. It opened up a whole new world for me. We got involved in meditation. I mean really really got into it. We studied it, got into something experts call sound-circles, which basically means we meditated in groups. We began going deeper and deeper into meditation, going into trances practically. At one point I ended up going into the bodies of animals, becoming them. The soft parts of my body would take the shape of different animals. My favorite was a shark—I loved to make shark faces." He made a few faces, his head moving eerily back and forth, his chin tucked in.

"I started going to the aquarium and learning more about sharks. I started—if you can believe it—kind of identifying with them. But over time, I found that I started to get fearful of animals. It was like I was starting to, like, *feel* their movement, . . . like for a moment I would become one. The scariest were spiders.

"Anyway, this was around 1992. Then came December 3, 1992. I remember it like it was yesterday. At three A.M. I woke up. I had a strange feeling—as if someone was contacting me. And out of nowhere, aliens jumped into my head. Just as if in my mind I knew I was being contacted by aliens. In the course of a month, I was able to contact them as well. They spoke through my body. If I had a strong muscle twitch it was yes; a weak one was no. I could have a two-way conversation without voices."

I asked Sam what they wanted.

"They said something was going to happen and I needed to

take a trip. They wanted me to hop into a truck and use kines-thesiology as direction. So I took off. I turned left onto 93 north, through North Conway to the Kankamangus Highway. Made a big loop. Then they said I was to pull off into a rest area. Then I heard a woman's voice, a high-pitched squeal. It was telling me that Pat, my wife, was the reincarnation of Jesus and I needed to kill her.

"I became very alarmed and agitated. Her higher self wanted me to kill her! I went home and told Pat something was wrong with my mind. They were contacting me, and I told her what they wanted. Then they started contacting me again with what they wanted. I was directed toward a gas station and was told to tell Pat, 'You're running away with the woman I love.' Then they told me to start yelling at cars and saying, 'Stop! The bridge is going to collapse—a big truck is coming!' But nothing happened.

"The aliens were making my legs shake. The police brought me to the hospital. They thought I was having a seizure, but the doctors found nothing medically wrong with me. Then they brought me to a psychiatrist who put me on antipsychotics. I was there for about two weeks. Pat came to visit me with her sister and daughter. But the entities told me to hit the guard, smash the window, and commit suicide. I can't remember the details, but they gave me more antipsychotics.

"During this time, the entities were telling me all kinds of things. I was supposed to teach the staff not to eat animals. The way I was supposed to do this was to spill my milk, get into a fetal ball on the floor, masturbate, and pee in my pants. Finally I just stopped. I was finally able to stop paying attention to what they wanted.

"So I was fine for a while. I still heard the entities, but I was able to not pay attention. I did have problems with my short-term memory, though. I lost my short-term memory for about three months. I do remember that Pat brought me to a Catholic diocese in January of the following year. They told me that I was speaking in tongues and that an exorcism was necessary. I can't really remember what happened, but around that time I stopped hearing the entities.

"The doctors all told me I had a mental problem, that I had to stay on the medication. My cousin has a mental problem—once she thought she was the baby Jesus. The doctor who saw me at the hospital wanted to write some medical paper on what happened to me, but I said *no*. He didn't understand what had happened—it was too advanced for Western medicine.

"You know, what happened to me is very anxiety-producing. Not a day goes by that I don't think about it. I just hope that something good comes from it."

Still reeling from my interview with Sam (who I hope is still taking his medication), I met with Laurie, a fifty-eight-year-old fitness instructor who lived in Cambridge. She was petite, trim, and dark-haired, with an easy smile and a reassuringly calm manner. She had a college degree, was divorced, and had three children between the ages of twenty-six and thirty-five.

"What happened to me—I don't know how to refer to the experience. I like to go out on the golf course behind my house at night. I like to look at the stars. It's beautiful and peaceful and it relaxes me. In September of 1999, I was standing where I always go, near the sixth tee, and then I saw something. I could see it in the distance, something wavery.

"There was a full moon out, but whatever it was cut the moon in half, blocked half of it, as if the moon had been folded back. I walked toward the place where it was. I felt as if I was underwater. I was fascinated, not afraid. Whatever it was seemed to come closer to me. It had a shape, but it was—what's the word? Well, you could see through it. I walked around the golf course for a while and it came with me, sort of floated next to me. But as soon as I left the golf course, it was gone. I wanted to wake up the kids and show them, but it was too late.

"Nothing like that had ever happened to me. I never really told anyone about it. Although I did see the movie *Contact*, aliens, UFOs, all that stuff has never been a special interest for me. It still isn't, really. I'm not sure what happened. I've studied physics and chemistry, but I really feel that it was alien contact I had that night. I had this overwhelming feeling of wonder and surprise."

My next subject lived in a tiny town in New Hampshire, and I drove there for our interview (it was the only way she was willing to participate in the study). It took me forty-five minutes to get within one mile of the house, and another forty-five minutes to find it—buried in the woods, surrounded by snowdrifts and pine trees and unpaved roads with no names. Peggy was thirty-six, divorced, an art teacher at a public school. She was tall, lanky, and fair-skinned, had a healthy, ruddy complexion, and looked as if she'd just returned from a morning of cross-country skiing, or modeling for the L. L. Bean winter catalog. She made me hot chocolate. I liked her. She seemed like a sensible, outdoorsy, independent woman, with no interest in alternative or New Age beliefs.

She told me that around the time she and her husband had been separating, she'd started having problems with anxiety and depression. "I was living alone for the first time in this house, and for some reason I started to have an unbelievable fear of looking at pictures of aliens. It started when *Close Encounters* came out, and got worse after I read Whitley Strieber's books. I really couldn't sleep. I was obsessing about having aliens around me. Then I started to have vivid dreams about aliens, grays. Somehow they wanted to buy land in New Hampshire, stay here, and breed. Sometimes I would wake up in the middle of the night screaming, but not making a noise. I'd be paralyzed, trying to scream, but I couldn't. My heart would be pounding. I'd be sweating. This still happens, like, once a month. It terrifies me.

"I am not a skeptic. I'm a believer. I wonder if they got me. I think that's why I wake up screaming. I think it happens at night. And when I wake up, I feel like I'm going to see one—a feeling like they're there, in the room, like I can see one. But I don't."

Jeff was a fifty-year-old construction worker from a middle-class suburb of Boston who had been out of work for several years as the result of an on-the-job back injury. He had a high school degree and had been married to the same woman for thirty years. Although he'd been raised in an Irish Catholic family and had attended parochial schools, he said firmly that he was no longer a practicing Catholic. "Forget organized religions—they're all cults."

"I don't know why I'm interested in aliens, but I have been since I was a kid. I read *Intruders*. No one else was into it like me. My wife found me this article about Budd Hopkins. . . . Now I watch anything I can about extraterrestrials—talk shows, movies, books, you name it. The stuff turns some people off; they say it's loony tunes. But not me.

"Sometimes I think we've all been abducted. These aliens—they're so advanced that we could be all part of an experiment. Maybe because of the atom bomb, they need to keep tabs on us. Global warming, cloning, the Apache helicopter. We're going to do it over and over again. That's why they're here—to protect us.

"I wonder if maybe I've been abducted and that's why I'm so interested in the stuff. When I was in Vegas with the wife, I wanted to go see Area 51, that secret military base.

"You know why people don't believe? Because nobody looks up. They don't see anything. People need to look up more, and then they'd believe. Two years ago I saw a star moving quickly from left to right. It was moving pretty good, real fast. A few minutes later, it came back and I saw it again. I think it was a UFO.

"Do I think I've been abducted? I really don't know. About a year ago, I was standing at the bathroom sink and I found a hole in my neck—there was some kind of lump in it. I squeezed it and something came out, something went clink in the sink and then went down the drain. I wish I'd seen it. I wish I still had it.

"Once, when I was younger, I was with a group of buddies at Fenway Park watching a game. We were drinking, horsing around, and things got a little fuzzy later on that night. Next thing I remember, I was on Mission Hill and it was five in the morning. I didn't know where I was; don't know how I got there. You hear how advanced they are—they could have just wiped it from my mind, whatever happened that night. Then there's the mystery of the Pyramids. Who do you think built them? The aliens helped to build them.

"You know, I believe we're all in a learning stage. There's a whole universe out there of stuff we know nothing about."

In short, consistent with other research conducted on alien abductees, this was an extremely varied group of people. It included construction workers and doctors, high school graduates and Ivy Leaguers, teenagers and grandfathers, yoga-oriented fitness types and depressed housewives, charismatic extroverts and introverted geeks, well-adjusted schoolteachers and homicidal psychiatric outpatients. The average age of the abductees I interviewed was forty-seven. That would put them in their twenties and thirties during the first cultural outbreaks of abductee reports in the 1970s and 1980s (for example, the Hills' made-for-TV movie, and Strieber's bestselling book *Communion*).

Consistent with Roy Baumeister's review of the data, the abductees in the study fit the description of white middle-class Americans (for the record, I never encountered a black abductee). The mean number of years of education was fifteen—no different from that of the control group.

Regrettably, I did not collect detailed data regarding religious background. Of the abductees in the study, 85 percent reported that they had been raised either Catholic or Protestant, approximately 10 percent had a Jewish upbringing, one was a Muslim, and one a Buddhist; the rest claimed no religious affiliation. Fewer than 10 percent were actually practicing any religion. If it were possible to go back and do the study again, I would have collected a measure of religiosity (how religious or spiritual these people felt, their need for religiosity or spirituality, and so on).

Aside from the fact that they all believed in aliens, did they have anything in common? Can we say anything conclusive about their psychiatric health, their personalities, or their cognitive functioning?

I think the answer is yes. First, aside from Al, they didn't appear to be seriously psychiatrically impaired. This doesn't mean that at some point in their lives, they, like the rest of us, hadn't sought or needed help for psychological problems or even met the criteria for a diagnosis. What it means is that the diagnosis wouldn't have explained their alien-abduction beliefs. There's little evidence that this was a particularly psychopathological group.[1]

But that being said, they were unusual in a couple of ways. For one thing, as a group they scored high on measures indicative of a personality construct called *schizotypy*. Schizotypy is not in itself abnormal, though it may indicate a "genetic marker" or a "genetic latent liability" for schizophrenia—a devastating psychiatric disorder characterized by delusions, hallucinations, and other forms of cognitive impairment.[2]

People who show signs of schizotypy are by no means schizophrenic, but they're generally a bit odd. They tend to look and think eccentrically and are prone to "magical" thinking and odd beliefs (for instance, that certain numbers have special powers, or that you can influence the future by thinking about it). They are often loners, and they typically believe in paranormal phenomena such as telepathy and clairvoyance.

Alien abductees score higher than nonbelievers on measures of schizotypy.[3] Does this mean that they tend to be crazier? No. At most, if symptoms of schizophrenia lie on a continuum, alien abductees are perhaps closer to being schizophrenic—that is, more inclined to magical thinking and perceptual aberration—than the average person.[4]

But that's still a bit of a guess, especially since the genetics of schizophrenia and schizotypy are still not well understood. At present, we have no neat psychiatric category that encompasses alien abductees. But if I had trained as a physician in the nineteenth century, the diagnosis would be easy: I'd say they were hysterical. Hysteria once described a psychological disorder—one in which unconscious desires or unexpressed emotions were supposedly converted into psychological symptoms and experiences. The diagnosis was quite popular in the late nineteenth century and during the heyday of psychoanalysis.

But around 1980 it was expunged from the formal diagnostic system.[5] What *are* unconscious desires, anyway? How do you measure unexpressed emotions? Today, if the word "hysteria" is used at all, it applies to certain behaviors and symptoms that produce the appearance of a disorder—of a "real condition"—although one that has no complete biomedical explanation. Some researchers claim that irritable-bowel syndrome, chronic-fatigue syndrome, and Gulf War syndrome are recent examples of hysteria.[6]

Alien abduction fits this profile, in that many abductees report trauma reactions as a result of their symptoms. They can't sleep at night; they're filled with terror; they can't concentrate. Some psychologists treat alien abductees for Post-Traumatic Stress Disorder, because many abductees meet the criteria for PTSD.[7] They have the requisite symptoms, such as reliving experiences, persistent emotional numbness, and hyperarousal. Replace "alien abduction" with "car accident" as the triggering event, and these people might legitimately take paid sick leave from their jobs.

Scholars of hysteria note that the primary reason we don't discuss it seriously as a psychological condition is that it is nearly impossible to develop a reliable diagnostic category to fit the vast set of behaviors and symptoms that hysterics report: from limps and blindness to stomach pain and nightmares. The symptoms of hysteria—their form and content—change through the decades. In the words of one historian, "The history of hysteria is not a single unbroken narrative but a scatter of occurrences. . . . Hysteria is a mimetic disorder—it mimics culturally permissible forms of disease."[8]

Hysterical illnesses are a function of their place and time. A man from North America can complain of nausea and fatigue related to the "yuppie flu" but not that his penis is retracting into his body, although the latter symptom would be acceptable in South China.[9] Recently, in northern Nicaragua, there was an outbreak of spirit possession which resulted in unfortunate side effects such as seizures and projectile vomiting. Local authorities, unconcerned with first-world diagnostic systems, knew how to treat the outbreak. They brought in shamans and *brujas* (witches), who were much more effective at providing treatment than medical doctors or psychotherapists. The outbreak was quelled in about three days. What better way to fight imaginary illnesses than with imaginary treatments?

Hysteria is alive and well in Nicaragua. In the United States, we've killed it by reclassifying many of its traditional symptoms into other disorders, such as somatization disorder and dissociative disorder. But while the terminology changes, the patients' experiences probably don't. When alien abductees are on their knees, rocking back and forth, weeping and crying out as they relive vivid memories of horrific sexual and medical experiences, they eerily resemble the hysterical patients that French physician Jean-Martin Charcot treated a century ago. They are expressing a culturally formed manifestation of human needs and conflicts.

What can we say about alien abductees and their personalities? They certainly seem to be particularly imaginative and prone to fantasy. Though we all have imaginations, people who are "fantasy prone" in the technical sense account for only about 4 percent of the population.[10] They have fertile imaginations, daydream a lot, and report very rich visual imagery, and some can achieve orgasm in the absence of any physical stimulation (a skill that should be taught). They enjoy art and music more deeply than other people, and have extremely vivid memories. In short, they are good at having compelling imaginative experiences—ones that feel as real as real. For all of these reasons, they are excellent hypnotic subjects. The link between fantasy-proneness and hypnotic susceptibility has been well documented.[11] And not surprisingly, people who believe they were abducted are more fantasy prone than others.[12]

And what about their memory functioning? Vivid and traumatic personal memories of being abducted by aliens have been primarily understood by academics as instances of "false-memory syndrome."[13] But what interested me was that although this hypothesis was common among psychological theorists, no one had actually tested it. Sure, it made *sense*—but were there any data to support it? Were alien abductees in fact particularly prone to creating false memories?

In 2002, my colleagues and I used a standardized laboratory paradigm to examine false-memory creation in alien abductees. It was quite similar to the paradigm we used to study false-memory creation in people reporting recovered memories of sexual abuse (an experiment described in Chapter 1). It involved a variant of a paradigm originally developed by James Deese in 1959 and modified by researchers in the 1990s.[14]

We asked three groups of people (those with alien-abduction memories, those who believed they'd been abducted by aliens but who had no actual memories, and those with no memories or beliefs of alien abduction—the control group) to study lists of words. Each list comprised words that were semantically related to each other *and* to another word (*not included* in the list) that we called the "nonpresented theme word." For example, one list consisted of words associated with the nonpresented theme word "sweet" (for example, "sour," "candy," "sugar," "bitter"). Following presentation of the list, subjects were asked to recall which words were on the list. False recall and false recognition (two examples of memory distortion) occurred when the subjects incorrectly remembered seeing the nonpresented theme word (in this case, "sweet").

The point of the experiment was simple: to find out whether alien abductees were more likely than controls to create false memories in the lab (that is, more likely to exhibit false recall and/or false recognition). Why was this important? Because if they *were* more prone to create false memories in the lab, this was broadly consistent with the idea that they would be more likely to create false memories outside the lab—in the real world—as well.

Several things clearly emerged from the experiment. First, the data were consistent with the idea that abductees were prone to creating false memories in the lab. They appeared to have trouble with source monitoring—that is (as mentioned in Chapter 3), they were likely to confuse things they had thought about and imagined with things they had actually seen, read, and heard in movies, books, or TV shows.[15]

When the research was written up and published, many abductees were incensed. One of the main criticisms was neatly summed up by one of John Mack's acolytes: "What the hell does studying lists of words have to do with alien abductions?" (Or as my advisor translated the complaint: "Ah! This gentleman has concerns about the ecological validity of the research!") Such research is relevant because if alien abductees are prone to creating false memories in the lab, there is no reason to believe they wouldn't tend to do so in the real world as well.

The data also indicated that there was, in general, a positive correlation between people's scores on measures of schizotypy and their scores on measures of fantasy-proneness. Typical symptoms of schizotypy: "Sometimes I dream about things before they happen"; "Some people can make me aware of them just by thinking about me"; "Sometimes I have feelings that I'm united with an object near me." Typical symptoms of fantasy-proneness: "When I listen to music, I get so caught up in it that I don't notice anything else"; "The crackle and flames of a wood fire stimulate my imagination"; "My thoughts often occur not as words but as visual images." The more symptoms of schizotypy and fantasy-proneness people reported, the more likely they were to create false memories in the lab. And who scored the highest on these two measures? People who believed they'd been abducted by aliens.

So what does this all mean? What can we say conclusively about this diverse group of abductees? In the end, not much. Research on the topic is clearly in its infancy. What we *can* confidently say is that these people are not crazy. They tend to have unusual ideas, experiences, and beliefs—ones that don't necessarily conform to mainstream social beliefs and tendencies. They believe not only in alien abduction, but also in things like ESP, astrology, tarot, channeling, auras, holistic medicine, and crystal therapy.

And they see themselves as different, unique, creative. Sometimes they are proud of their perceived differences ("That's why I
was chosen—I'm different from most people . . . special, you could
say"). But often they feel alienated ("I always knew I was different.
. . . I feel as though my real family is somewhere else").

If we accept that about 4 percent of the population is fantasy
prone, and that fantasy-proneness correlates with schizotypy,
there are probably about 18 million Americans who fit this profile. Very few of them believe they've been abducted. But they are
likely to believe in other weird phenomena—ghosts, past lives,
multiple personalities. If you want to meet such people, I can tell
you that they gravitate to certain professions—for instance, massage therapy, yoga instruction, the theater, the visual arts. You can
find them in the New Age section of bookstores, at open-mike po-
etry readings, and in health food stores. They may well be dressed
in purple or buying incense.

But remember that a rich fantasy life, magical beliefs, and
strange perceptual symptoms are not in themselves enough to
make people think they were abducted. What is also required is a
belief system—one that predisposes them to interpret unusual experiences and thoughts in terms of an extraterrestrial hypothesis,
rather than, say, multiple personalities or chronic-fatigue syndrome or attention deficit disorder. Researchers have hypnotized
control subjects and asked them to vividly imagine experiences
they had in a past life. Not surprisingly, the fantasy-prone individuals generated them. But just because people can generate a past-
life experience doesn't mean they'll actually believe in it. Only
those subjects who *already* thought that reincarnation was a real
possibility were likely to believe in what they imagined.[16]

For more than a decade, I have worked with a great variety of people who had strange beliefs and false memories. Some believed that they were victims of satanic cults, some that they had multiple personalities, some that they'd been abducted by aliens. What they all had in common was, first, a tendency to fantasize and to hold unusual belief and ideas; and, second, a rash of disturbing experiences (sleep paralysis, anxiety, relationship problems) for which they were seeking an explanation. But they differed in the culturally available explanation they chose. For the group at the center of this book, alien abduction was the best fit for their symptoms and experiences. It was a credible enough explanation for them to seek out a hypnotist, in order to recover—or create—their memories.

6 If It Didn't Happen, Why Would I Want To Believe It Did?

Are people being abducted by aliens? No. In 1969 the National Academy of Sciences sponsored a study of all the available evidence on UFOs. The conclusion: "On the basis of present knowledge, the least likely explanation of unidentified flying objects is the hypothesis of extraterrestrial visitations by intelligent beings."[1] Nothing has changed since then. To date, there is no objective evidence that an alien spacecraft has ever visited Earth or that anyone has ever been abducted.[2]

Believers always ask me whether I think that life exists elsewhere in the universe, but the question isn't really relevant to the credibility of alien-abduction claims. It's one thing to believe that life might exist on other planets, and quite another to believe that it is secretly examining your private parts.

Sometimes I try to argue back. If there are so many planets that could support life, then where are the aliens? Billions of dollars have been spent trying to find some, but so far no ET has phoned our home. If they *must* be out there, then why haven't we seen them yet?[3] Unfortunately, this line of argument leads nowhere with believers, because the answer is always the same: "Some of us *have* seen them! You're just not taking us seriously."

This book has tried to do just that: to take alien-abduction accounts seriously, but not literally. I began by pointing out that psychologists were slow to devote their thoughts and research efforts to understanding how sane people can come to believe they were abducted by aliens. At last, in the 1990s, explanations and theories began to appear.[4] But while I applaud and have drawn on this growing body of research, I do think there's a self-congratulatory tone to much of it—a sense that the whole ridiculous issue of aliens has now been addressed and answered, and can be dismissed as another example of mass foolishness.

Though individual researchers naturally incline toward their own explanations for the alien-abduction experience (it's mostly sleep paralysis, says Richard McNally; it's memory distortion, says Elizabeth Loftus; it's fantasy-proneness, say Robert Bartholomew and George Howard),[5] I would hope they'd be receptive to my multilevel synthesis of these disparate contributions. I am arguing that alien-abduction memories are best understood as resulting from a blend of fantasy-proneness, memory distortion, culturally available scripts, sleep hallucinations, and scientific illiteracy, aided and abetted by the suggestions and reinforcement of hypnotherapy. But this analysis is still insufficient for an understanding of the phenomenon. As the abductees themselves would say, "If you're telling me it didn't happen to me, that I made it up, why in God's name would I *want* to?"

That's the hardest question to answer. The experiences are terrifying, nightmarish. They take place in the dark when you're alone and vulnerable. The alien creatures are repulsive, with vacant black eyes, long fingers, segmented bodies. They steal you away from all that's safe and familiar, and then they probe and dig into your brains, nasal cavities, genitals, and intestines. Things are carved out of you, or embedded in you. Even if it seems reasonable to accept the explanatory equation presented above and acknowledge that false beliefs *can* be created, it's difficult to understand *why* anyone would make up such ghastly things. David Jacobs, a leading researcher in the field, argues that abduction narratives "would be extremely difficult, if not impossible, to attribute to internally generated psychological fantasies." John Mack, in a memorable phrase, called the typical account "a self-destroying traumatic narrative."[6]

One theory, proposed by the social psychologist Roy Baumeister and treated in an entire issue of the prestigious journal *Psychological Inquiry* (1996), is that alien abductees are masochists. They *like* the pain of the experience; they "get off" on it. In response to stress, anxiety, the myriad slings and arrows of life (goes the theory), some people develop the urge to escape from themselves periodically; experiences that undermine self-esteem and thwart control may help them to strip away "the burdensome conceptions of selfhood."[7] So the urges that make some people masochists (their craving for pain, their wish to be humiliated— desires so strong that they will pay to have them gratified) are perhaps also expressed in abduction accounts. Another theory, endorsed by more than a few, is that abductees are just "little nobodies seeking celebrity status."[8]

Neither of these theories holds much explanatory power— which is not surprising, since their advocates have probably never actually talked to any abductees. Of course, some abductees probably do relish the opportunity to escape the "burdensome conceptions of selfhood," and others are certainly desperate for attention; but this fact doesn't explain the actual belief. Though psychologists are to be commended for beginning to address the question of how ordinary people come to believe extraordinary things, they are still largely tone deaf to the purposes that these beliefs serve for the individuals who hold them. Proponents of such explanations are missing something profoundly important about abduction belief—perhaps the most salient factor underlying its formation: people's desire to find meaning for their lives.

In Chapter 2, I argued that one appealing aspect of the belief is that it provides abductees with an explanation for distressing, disturbing, confusing experiences and emotions. The seed of the alien-abduction belief is always a question. Such questions can seem small and insignificant: "Why did I wake up in the middle of the night unable to move?" "Why do I have frequent nightmares?" "What are these strange coin-shaped marks on my back?" "Why was I compelled to drive twenty-five miles out of the city last night?" Or they are profound and important: "Why do I feel so alone?" "Why am I different from everyone else?" "Why are my relationships so rocky?" "Why do I feel empty and depressed all the time?" The questions lead to a search for causes, and then, eventually, to belief in alien abduction.

Richard Ofshe and Ethan Watters studied the motivational factors behind false belief of another kind—namely, belief in childhood sexual abuse.[9] They are widely cited for popularizing Frederic Bartlett's 1932 "effort after meaning" hypothesis.[10] Specifically, they argued that women with unexplained psychological distress are trying to find meaning for their anguish and seize upon the sexual-abuse explanation as a magic bullet. Not surprisingly, this is an extremely unpopular research topic—which is a bit ironic because Sigmund Freud, a hero to some of the therapists and researchers who dislike this line of research, was probably the first to discuss and endorse the idea.

Freud has been much criticized since the mid-1990s. His research methods have been attacked, his conclusions derided as illogical, his theories dismissed as flawed.[11] He was clearly no scientist.[12] But if we think of Freud as a philosopher rather than as a psychologist, we can be grateful for at least one enormous contribution to the behavioral sciences: he was perhaps the first to perceive and understand how people's mental health can benefit when they are able to create a coherent narrative for their lives. Freud's so-called analytic technique was actually a process of synthesis, of composition. He would sit down with individuals who were suffering from psychological distress and would listen to them, with enormous patience, in an effort to discover the complexity and history of their mental state. And during the months or years of therapy, he would take the previously disconnected pieces of his patients' lives—dreams, phobias, emotions, childhood memories—and weave them together into a story that made sense to them (or more importantly to him, as his critics would say), a story that persuasively explained to these patients the psychological distress they were experiencing.

Freud may well have been the first to discover that creating a theory or having an explanation for current problems or distress can be comforting for many: it's a way to make sense of apparently random pain. It's generally why people seek psychotherapy today—not just because they want to get rid of symptoms, whether panic attacks or compulsive behaviors or depression, but they want to know *why* they're having these problems in the first place. Understanding the reasons for our emotions—and creating an explanatory narrative—is, for many of us, very important.

But are the explanations we come up with correct? Do we feel depressed or have bad dreams or fail at life tasks because we were emotionally neglected by our parents? Or—as Freud initially claimed and as many psychotherapists still believe—because we were sexually abused as children? Or because we've been denied access to our hybrid alien children? Depending on the book we're reading or the guests on the talk show we're currently watching, we can choose from countless ways to reframe, reconceptualize, and understand our past. But are any of them right?

The psychiatrist and psychoanalyst Donald Spence brilliantly addressed this topic in his book *Narrative Truth and Historical Truth*. The narrative structures we impose on our lives, either in therapy or on our own, are, unsurprisingly, not always accurate: they reflect our preexisting beliefs, biases, and prejudices, including ones we may not even know we have. "Believing that the narratives we create to explain our distress accurately reflect reality is both optimistic and naive." The idea that a patient is an unbiased reporter of his or her experiences and the therapist an unbiased listener, and that together they are engaged in an archaeological exploration expedition of the past, runs counter to everything memory researchers know about the malleable, unstable nature of memory and especially about the way our memories are altered by our expectations and feelings.[13]

But Spence also argues that the validity of our conclusions—the *historical* truth of our explanations—is irrelevant. The important question is: Do our beliefs have *narrative* truth? Do they provide us with meaning and value? When people believe they were abducted by aliens, does this help them to understand perplexing or upsetting aspects of their lives? If so, the explanation is going to be persuasive, satisfying, and resistant to argument.

This was definitely the case with my alien abductees. All of them, prior to recovering their memories, had sought out books, movies, researchers, and hypnotists in an effort to understand the things that were troubling them—why they couldn't sleep at night, felt estranged from other people, had sexual difficulties, had strange marks on their bodies, felt urges to drink or take drugs.

"I never knew who I was. I knew I felt different, but not why. It was as if the whole world was going by me and I could only silently watch, observe. I was never part of it. Now I understand that I'm different, and this makes everything fall into place."

"I couldn't be touched—not even by my husband, who's a kind and gentle man. Imagine being forty-five and not knowing what good sex was! Now I understand that it's related to what the beings did to me. I was a sexual experiment to them from an early age."

"Oh God, was there anything I didn't try? You name it and I did it. Drugs, alcohol, sexual addiction, eating—believe me, I tried them all. There was just something missing from my life. I was empty because I didn't know why I was . . . what the point of everything was. I was empty, looking to be filled up by something else. Now that I have my memories, I understand why. Everything makes a lot more sense to me now."

It probably doesn't much matter to the abductees whether they're right or wrong. They simply feel better because of what they believe.

I am certainly not the first to argue that believing weird things confers benefits on the believers by providing explanations for psychological problems and general unhappiness. Keith Thomas, for example, says this in his influential book on medieval magical beliefs—astrology, witchcraft, Catholicism. His widely accepted conclusion was that these examples of pseudo-science "offered an explanation for misfortune, a means of redress in times of uncertainty." And this statement is equally relevant to today's belief in alien abduction and any number of other weird phenomena. The beliefs may be different, Thomas wrote, but the central feature of all of them is a preoccupation with the explanation and relief of human misfortune.[14]

Moreover, when people find an explanation for their distress, it often seems to absolve them of responsibility for that distress. No contemporary "magical belief" better exemplifies this than the belief in multiple-personality disorder (MPD), a popular diagnosis in the 1980s and 1990s. The hypnosis researcher Nicholas Spanos argued not only that multiple personalities were a social construct, but that many people derived advantages from a situation in which they had competing personalities vying for control of their actions. Their behavior, they could claim, wasn't their fault but the fault of their alter egos, and was the result of a history of childhood abuse that they'd completely forgotten. Since they weren't in control of their behavior, they weren't responsible for their lives: they were the victims of a past that had been inflicted on them.[15] Corbett Thigpen and Hervey Cleckley, authors of the book *The Three Faces of Eve* (the Rosetta Stone of MPD), wryly commented that "many reported MPD patients today appear primarily motivated by the secondary gain of avoiding responsibility."[16] This finds a close echo in the words of one abductee, whose attitude was quite typical: "I don't focus too much on what's going on today anymore—the here and now. I don't care. What I do doesn't matter too much. We're not in control of our lives anyway."

Explaining psychological distress and avoiding responsibility for misfortune are certainly desirable goals for many people. Every single abductee at some point during an interview said, "Things make sense now." But is this enough to explain the appeal of the alien-abduction narrative? It makes sense that people reach for explanations and excuses to mitigate the harshness of their lives, but do the explanations have to be so strange? There are many other, more acceptable ways for people to explain their problems. Just turn on the TV and watch some talk shows; or, better yet, browse through the self-help and psychology sections of any bookstore. The variety of proposed explanations for personal problems is dizzying: attention deficit disorder, alcoholic parents, neglect of the inner child, depression of a spouse, a surfeit of carbohydrates, a deficiency of protein, the stresses of being unmarried, an overly rigid sense of morality, societal pressure to be good-looking, the plight of being a middle child, a history of sexual abuse, and on and on. The awareness and acceptance of such explanations are amazingly widespread. Recently I asked an elderly neighbor why she still smoked. Although she's ninety-one, has lived in Nicaragua her whole life, speaks no English, and has a fourth-grade education, she turned to me confidently and said: "It's not my fault. I have an addictive personality."

With such a wealth of choices, why do people continue to blame creepy, repulsive, terrifying aliens? In part because once they develop memories of abduction—which confirm all their vague suspicions—they find it hard to *disbelieve*. Human memory is fallible, hypnosis exacerbates source-monitoring problems, and vivid and powerful memories emerge—memories that feel too real to be explained in conventional ways. Yet even if abductees could get rid of these powerful and frightening new memories, most of them wouldn't want to.

The memories are powerful not just because they feel real, but also because something profound happens to the individuals who "recover" them—something that is immune to logic or appeals to probability, something that is intense and emotional.

"I know you think it sounds weird. Everyone does. What happened to me was—overwhelming. It was more real than my sitting here talking with you right now. It . . . felt sense-making. . . . I can't explain it—but I don't have to. All I can say is that it happened to me; it didn't happen to you. I felt it."

"I don't care that it doesn't make sense to you, or that scientists say it can't happen. It did. I was taken. It happened to me and nothing has been the same. I was changed, and I know it's true."

The contact these people have had with aliens doesn't just feel real—it feels transformative.

In one study I worked on (mentioned in Chapter 3), abductees were asked to write about their most traumatic experiences. The goal was to examine how their bodies reacted to memories of those horrific events. Were their physiological reactions (heart rate, sweating) similar to those of other trauma victims, such as war vets and hurricane survivors? Excerpts from the abductees' written narratives were played back to them when they were "hooked up" in the lab, and their physiological responses were recorded and analyzed.[17]

We didn't just elicit trauma memories. We also asked subjects to write about their happiest experiences (weddings, graduations) and some emotionally neutral experiences (eating a meal; riding on a bus). These additional scripts served as necessary controls: we couldn't interpret the meaning of subjects' reactions to frightening scripts unless we could see how they responded to happy and boring memories as well. After all, what if the abductees got worked up over memories of alien abduction *and* memories of eating tuna-fish sandwiches? In that case, even if the subjects had a heart attack while listening to their abduction scripts, we wouldn't have learned much—except that they were highly emotional people in general.

During the writing part of the experiment, something happened that I didn't anticipate. All of the subjects reported that the most traumatic experiences in their lives were abduction-related. This was no surprise. But some of them also reported that their most *positive* life experiences were abduction-related as well. I had been involved with psychophysiology research for quite a while—had worked with all kinds of different trauma populations—but no subjects had ever told me that their best experience and their worst experience had been the same event. Can you imagine the victim of a car accident claiming that the best thing that ever happened to him was crashing through that median barrier, upside down, at eighty miles per hour?

I remember reading my first such narrative. In essence, it said: "The most positive event in my life was a contact experience. It included a journey into the core of source-consciousness, a realm of infinite light. Here I felt the ultimate sensation of love without jealousy, desire without deceit. The sensation was intense. It enabled me to reevaluate the quality of my life—helped me to embrace and appreciate all the pain and ugliness that had ever happened to me. It helped me to see life as beautiful, as a gift."

I confess that at first I had absolutely no scientific curiosity about this type of response. Endorsing an alien-abduction experience as a positive event (in a study where it was assumed to be only a negative event) was not only annoying theoretically; it was profoundly disruptive to my research schedule. It was difficult enough to book lab space, coordinate with the techs who worked the electrode equipment, persuade the subjects to sign consent forms, get them to show up (a standard query from prospective subjects: "Does it involve electrodes?"), then ferry them to the lab in New Hampshire—an hour's drive. And now this! The subjects' happiest experience was not supposed to be flip side of their worst. We'd never had a Vietnam vet tell us that getting his leg blown off by a land mine was a great thing. Alien abductions are *traumatic*—they cause anguish, terror, and pain. How can they simultaneously be a "beautiful gift"?

Today, I realize that my initial response to these counter-intuitive data was not only immature and unprofessional, but profoundly unscientific. The best part of science, the thing that makes it work, is the fact that it is impartial and unbiased. It doesn't care what you want; it cares only about the truth. Science is a process of inquiry aimed at building knowledge—testable knowledge that is constantly open to rejection. I had to acknowledge the truth that was revealed in the evidence: the abductees had derived profound benefits from their dreadful experiences.

I was struck by the fact that all of the subjects, without exception, said that they felt "changed" because of their experiences, that "they were better people," that "life improved" after they were abducted. What was it about abduction that *felt right* to them? That was so awe-inspiring? People went so far as to say: "I would be much different if I hadn't been abducted. I would have led a much emptier, drier existence. Imagine we're all people standing on a beach. When you get your ankles wet, you realize there's a whole reality out there you didn't know about, so much you never even *knew.*" And: "The journey has enabled me to discover my place in the universe. I had felt abandoned, reduced to nothing but a sperm sample. Yet today I feel a tremendous expansiveness. In my total aloneness, I have discovered a oneness with the beings." And: "I know it sounds crazy, but the essence of it is that it changed my life. It taught me that we are not alone here. It made a better person out of me."

At the end of every interview, throughout the five-year course of the research, each abductee was asked the same question: "If you could do it all over again, would you choose *not* to be abducted?" No one ever said yes. Despite the shock and terror that accompanied their experiences, the abductees were glad to have had them. Their lives improved. They were less lonely, more hopeful about the future, felt they were better people. They chose abduction.

Being abducted by aliens is a transformative event. Not only does it furnish an explanation for psychological distress and unsettling experiences; it provides meaning for one's entire life. As abductees have said, it "enlarged my world view," "gave me wisdom to share," "caused me to care about the spiritual path of mankind," "expanded my reality." The beauty of the abduction belief is that it doesn't just explain specific problems, like headaches and sexual dysfunction. It offers a comprehensive view of the world, an explanation for human existence, and the promise of a better life. Not surprisingly, once you "discover your place in the universe," you have a hard time being a skeptic.

Carl Sagan once said that people embrace pseudo-science in direct proportion to the degree to which they misunderstand science.[18] I started out this research project agreeing with him—but today I respectfully disagree. The abductees taught me that people go through life trying on belief systems for size. Some of these belief systems speak to powerful emotional needs that have little to do with science—the need to feel less alone in the world, the desire to have special powers or abilities, the longing to know that there is something out there, something more important than you that's watching over you. Belief in alien abduction is not just bad science. It's not just an explanation for misfortune and a way to avoid taking responsibility for personal problems. For many people, belief in alien abduction gratifies spiritual hungers. It reassures them about their place in the universe and their own significance.

If we act for a moment like anthropologists and examine the way in which such beliefs function, we see that they're really not about science at all. Rather than labeling them pseudo-science, let's call them a form of skepticism (one of the guiding principles of science). They emerge out of a dissatisfaction with conventional values and perspectives—a refusal to accept the way things are. In fact, if we situate these beliefs in their historical, social, and cultural context they seem less a turn toward irrationalism and more an idiom through which some people express their conflicts, desires, and needs.

So although in some ways I agree with Jung ("These people are lacking not only in criticism but in the most elemental knowledge of psychology; at bottom, they don't want to be taught any better but merely to go on believing"), I've turned away from this sort of supercilious tone.[19] We live in an age of science—of data, facts, experiments, and experts. The fact that pseudo-scientific beliefs are

proliferating more than ever clearly indicates that, for many people, science just isn't working. It is failing to meet their needs,
concerns, and longings.

Science demands reason, argument, rigorous standards of evidence and of honesty. These qualities make it the best knowledge-
gathering instrument we have, but they're also the reason it leaves
many people cold. Its methods are stodgy and grumpy; you must
prove your case in the face of determined, expert criticism; diver-
sity and debate are valued. The most we can hope for are suc-
cessive improvements in our understanding, the chance to learn
from our mistakes. Absolute certainty will always elude us. Nothing is ever known for sure, and there are no sacred truths.

But what if we *want* sacred truths? In the quest to find truth
and meaning for our lives, many of us, perhaps most of us, are
capable of abandoning skepticism, of deceiving ourselves, of in-
flating the possibilities in our abductive-reasoning equation. The
stories we tell ourselves are not simply a consequence of dispassionately applying theory to data; they're a function of what we
want to believe. Motivational and emotional considerations as
well as intellectual factors are involved in the construction of
autobiographical narratives. Our personal stories are inextricably linked to our needs, goals, and desires.[20] Alien-abduction accounts reveal that many of us want contact with something beyond human experience: contact with something supernatural,
with the divine.

I would have liked to stay away from the topic of religion in
this book—not just because I'm tired of dealing with controversial
issues, but also because I have about a thousand devout Irish
Catholic relatives I don't want to upset. Yet I can't avoid the subject. The parallels between the abduction experience and the age-

old Christian narrative are striking. Alien abductions feature all-knowing, nonhuman, advanced entities whose presence resists the explanatory power of science. The entities bring moral guidance. They tell us that time is running out, that we must change our selfish ways or our planet will be destroyed. They have come to Earth for our sake, and they are working for humanity's redemption. They want to produce superior beings. They seek not the union of God and man in Christ, but the union of aliens and humans in the hybrid. Religious creeds and UFO beliefs both require obeisance to a higher power—a power that must be accepted *on faith.*

Sometimes, on hearing a particularly graphic depiction of alien abduction, I get a haunting mental image of Bernini's *Saint Theresa and the Angel.*[21] I hate this sculpture. The grotesque mixture of pain and ecstasy on her face as she reels backward, having been pierced by a giant spear, is alarmingly provocative.

This sculpture depicts what is perhaps the most famous visitation recorded in Christian history. In 1562, Saint Theresa of Avila encountered an angel. "In his hands I saw a great golden spear and, at the iron tip, there appeared to be a point of fire. Then he plunged it into my heart several times, so that it penetrated my entrails. When he pulled it out, I felt that he took them with it, and left me utterly consumed with the great love of God. The pain was so severe it made me utter several moans. The sweetness caused by this intense pain is so extreme that one cannot possibly wish it to cease, nor is one's soul then content with anything but God. This is not a physical but a spiritual pain. So gentle is this wooing, which takes place between God and the soul, that if anyone thinks I am lying, I pray God, in His goodness, to grant him some experience of it."[22]

Compare this account with that of the famous alien visitation described by Betty Andreasson and quoted earlier, in Chapter 4. "What are you doing that for? What is that? . . . They are getting ready to do something. . . . They are doing something there. . . . They are preparing. Now they are pulling something. That needle again, with a tube, like, on the end. They are pulling—it looks like he's going to put it in me. Oh! And he's opening up my shirt, and—he's going to put that thing in my navel. Ohhhh, I don't like this! . . . Stop it! . . . Oh! He's pushing that around again, feeling things. I don't like this! . . . He's starting to take the thing out. Ohhhhh. Ahhhhh." At another point in her abduction, she comments: "I'm thinking they must be angels, and the Scriptures keep coming into my mind." She says an alien told her, "I have chosen you." Her awed response was, "Are you my Lord Jesus? I would recognize my Lord Jesus. I love you. God is love and I love you. . . . Oh, praise God, praise God! I know I am not worthy."[23]

Since the 1960s, countless abductees have said they are "thankful" they've been "chosen," they "feel less alone," they feel "blessed" because of their experiences. Yet Budd Hopkins, who has been researching and writing about abductions for many years, still asks: "Why would anyone fantasize a thing like this? It doesn't give you the satisfaction of having been chosen for some wonderful quasi-religious role in the world. In fact, you've been turned into a kind of neutered powerless figure with no autonomy whatever."[24] I have to wonder: Is he deaf?

"Obviously the abduction experiences were terrifying," said one abductee. "But after I was placed back in bed, I felt relieved and glad to have been taken. Again and again, I was overwhelmed by the feeling of . . . transformation. I feel very blessed to have been abducted. I have wisdom to share now. I'm interested in learning more about others. I guess the experience broadened my perceptions of what reality encompasses. It taught me that we are not here alone, and so my priorities in life have changed. I'm not hung up any more on earthly things. I care more about the spiritual path of mankind. All the hardships and suffering I've had to go through—they still hurt when I think about them, but I don't get angry anymore. I accept that this is what I had to go through to get here, to this point in my life. . . . These beings are like God's angels, in a very roundabout way—like messengers. They're here to expand our reality. They want to help us. Out of my aloneness, I have discovered oneness with the universe."

The primary lesson I learned from my research with abductees is that many of us long for contact with the divine, and aliens are a way of coming to terms with the conflict between science and religion. I agree with Jung: extraterrestrials are technological angels.[25]

It's clear that people get from their abduction beliefs the same things that millions of people the world over derive from their religions: meaning, reassurance, mystical revelation, spirituality, transformation. Frankly, I wish I had some. Alien-abduction beliefs can be considered a type of religious creed, based on faith, not facts. Indeed, a vast body of scientific data indicates that the believers are psychologically benefiting: they're happier, healthier, and more optimistic about their lives than people who lack such beliefs. We live in an age when science and technology prevail and traditional religions are under fire. Doesn't it make sense to wrap our angels and gods in space suits and repackage them as aliens?

We yearn for spiritualism and comfort, magic and meaning. As

Bertolt Brecht said in his play *Galileo,* we need something "to reassure us that the pageant of the world has been written around us, . . . that a part for us has been created beyond this wretched one on a useless star."[26] Being abducted by aliens may be a baptism into the new religion of our technological age.

Notes

Introduction

1. John Grant Fuller, *The Interrupted Journey: Two Lost Hours "Aboard a Flying Saucer"* (New York: Dial, 1966). Whitley Strieber, *Communion: A True Story* (New York: Avon, 1987). John E. Mack, *Abduction: Human Encounters with Aliens* (New York: Ballantine, 1995; orig. pub. 1994).
2. G. Gallup and F. Newport, "Belief in Paranormal Phenomena among Adult Americans," *Skeptical Inquirer,* 15 (1991): 137–147. J. Chequers, S. Joseph, and D. Diduca, "Belief in Extraterrestrial Life, UFO-Related Beliefs, and Schizotypal Personality," *Personality and Individual Differences,* 23 (1997): 519–521.
3. Anonymous, "Poll: U.S. Hiding Knowledge of Aliens," June 15, 1997, CNN Interactive, edition.cnn.com/US/9706/15/ufo.poll (accessed April 2005).
4. D. J. Coon, "Testing the Limits of Sense and Science: American Experimental Psychologists Combat Spiritualism, 1880–1920," *American Psychologist,* 47 (1992): 143–151. L. S. Newman and R. F. Baumeister, "Toward an Elaboration of the UFO Abduction Phenomenon: Hypnotic Elaboration, Extraterrestrial Sadomasochism, and Spurious Memories," *Psychological Inquiry,* 7 (1996): 99–126.
5. John E. Mack, *A Prince of Our Disorder: The Life of T. E. Lawrence* (Boston: Little, Brown, 1976).
6. John E. Mack, "A Wily Reality: Towards a Science of Human Experience," Report of a Two-Day Multidisciplinary Meeting on the Alien Abduction Phenomenon and Anomalous Experiences, Program for Extraordinary Experience Research (PEER), Harvard University, Spring 2000.
7. John E. Mack, *Passport to the Cosmos: Human Transformation and Alien Encounters* (New York: Crown, 1999).
8. Kaja Perina, "Cracking the Harvard X-Files," *Psychology Today* (March–April 2003): 62ff. Online version entitled "Alien Abductions: The Real Deal?" cms.psychologytoday.com/articles/pto-20030527-000002.html (accessed April 2005).
9. Chequers, Joseph, and Diduca, "Belief in Extraterrestrial life." S. A.

Clancy, R. J. McNally, D. L. Schacter, M. F. Lenzenweger, and R. J. Pitman, "Memory Distortion in People Reporting Abduction by Aliens," *Journal of Abnormal Psychology,* 111, no. 3 (2002): 455–461. C. C. McLeod, M. L. O'Connell, R. L. Colasanti, and J. E. Mack, "Anomalous Experience and Psychopathology: The Questions of Alien Abduction," unpublished manuscript. N. P. Spanos, C. A. Burgess, M. F. Burgess, "Past-Life Identities, UFO Abductions, and Satanic Ritual Abuse: The Social Construction of 'Memories,'" *International Journal of Clinical and Experimental Hypnosis,* 42 (1994): 433–446.

10. G. G. Sparks and W. Miller, "Investigating the Relationship between Exposure to Television Programs That Depict Paranormal Phenomena and Beliefs in the Paranormal," *Communication Monographs,* 68 (2001): 98–113. G. G. Sparks, C. W. Sparks, and K. Gray, "Media Impact on Fright Reactions and Belief in UFOs: The Potential Role of Mental Imagery," *Communication Research,* 22 (1995): 3–23.

11. Michael Shermer, *Why People Believe Weird Things: Pseudoscience, Superstition, and Other Confusions of Our Time* (New York: Freeman, 1997). Carl Sagan, *The Demon-Haunted World: Science as a Candle in the Dark* (New York: Ballantine, 1997; orig. pub. 1996). "Complete and utter nonsense": Murray Gell-Mann, cited in Shermer, *Why People Believe Weird Things,* 172.

12. Steven J. Dick, *Plurality of Worlds: The Origins of the Extraterrestrial Life Debate from Democritus to Kant* (Cambridge: Cambridge University Press, 1982). Michael J. Crowe, *The Extraterrestrial Life Debate, 1750–1990* (Mineola, N.Y.: Dover, 1999; orig. pub. 1986). Keith Thomas, *Religion and the Decline of Magic* (New York: Scribner, 1971).

13. Sagan, *The Demon-Haunted World,* 39, 5.

14. Jodi Dean, *Aliens in America: Conspiracy Cultures from Outerspace to Cyberspace* (Ithaca: Cornell University Press, 1998).

1.   How Do You Wind Up Studying Aliens?

1. For an excellent review, see Richard J. McNally, *Remembering Trauma* (Cambridge, Mass.: Harvard University Press, 2003).

2. M. Garry, C. G. Manning, E. F. Loftus, and S. J. Sherman, "Imagination Inflation: Imagining a Childhood Event Inflates Confidence That It Occurred," *Psychonomic Bulletin and Review,* 3 (1996): 208–214.

3. S. A. Clancy, R. J. McNally, and D. L. Schacter, "Effects of Guided Imagery on Memory Distortion in Women Reporting Recovered Memories of Childhood Sexual Abuse," *Journal of Traumatic Stress,* 12 (1999): 559–569.

4. S. A. Clancy, D. L. Schacter, R. J. McNally, and R. K. Pittman, "False Recognition in Women Reporting Recovered Memories of Sexual Abuse," *Psychological Science,* 11 (2000): 26–31.

5. Quoted by Diana Jean Schemo, *New York Times,* December 18, 2002.

6. See John E. Mack, "A Wily Reality: Towards a Science of Human Experience," Report of a Two-Day Multidisciplinary Meeting on the Alien Abduction Phenomenon and Anomalous Experiences, Program for Extraordinary Experience Research (PEER), Harvard University, Spring 2000.

7. At the request of some people affiliated with John Mack's research, the ad was subsequently reworded and made more politically correct: "Are you an experiencer?" The number of calls immediately decreased. The ad was then changed to read: "Seeking people who may have been contacted or abducted by space aliens, to participate in a memory study."

8. The fourteenth-century English philosopher and Franciscan monk William of Occam (or Ockham) did not originate the principle of parsimony ("Pluralitas non est ponenda sine necessitate"—"Plurality should not be posited without necessity"), but he used it so often in his writings that it has become associated with him. It's sometimes rendered: "What is done with fewer assumptions is done in vain with more." In other words, the simplest explanation that fits the facts is the one that should be chosen.

2.   How Do People Come To Believe They Were Abducted By Aliens?

1. S. Blackmore, "Abduction by Aliens or Sleep Paralysis?" *Skeptical Inquirer,* 22, no. 3 (1998): 23–28. J. A. Cheyne, I. R. Newby-Clark, and S. D. Rueffer, "Relations among Hypnogogic and Hypnopompic Experiences Associated with Sleep Paralysis," *Journal of Sleep Research,* 8 (1999): 313–317. J. Allan Hobson, *Sleep* (New York: Scientific American Library, 1995). K. J. Holdon and C. C. French "Alien Abduction Experiences: Some Clues from Neuropsychology and Neuropsychiatry," *Cognitive Neuropsychiatry,* 7 (2002): 163–178. David J. Hufford, *The Terror That Comes in the Night: An Experience-Centered Study of Supernatural Assault Traditions* (Philadelphia: University of Pennsylvania Press, 1982). R. J. McNally and S. A. Clancy, "Sleep Paralysis, Sexual Abuse, and Space Alien Abduction," *Transcultural Psychiatry,* 42 (2005): 113–122.

2. M. Kottmeyer, "Gauche Encounters: Bad Films and the UFO Mythos," Unpublished manuscript, 1989. Idem, "The Eyes That Spoke," *Skeptical Briefs Newsletter,* 4 (1994). Terry Matheson, *Alien Abductions: Creating a Modern Phenomenon* (Amherst, N.Y.: Prometheus Books, 1998). John

F. Moffitt, *Picturing Extraterrestrials: Alien Images in Modern Culture* (Amherst, N.Y.: Prometheus Books, 2003).

3. Budd Hopkins, *Missing Time* (New York: Berkley, 1983). Matheson, *Alien Abductions*. John E. Mack, *Abduction: Human Encounters with Aliens* (New York: Ballantine, 1995; orig. pub. 1994). John Grant Fuller, *The Interrupted Journey: Two Lost Hours "Aboard a Flying Saucer"* (New York: Dial, 1966).

4. SETI stands for Search for Extraterrestrial Intelligence. The SETI Institute, founded in 1984, is a private, nonprofit organization dedicated to scientific research, education, and public outreach. Carl Sagan was a past director.

5. S. Koenig, "Close Encounters, Close by," *Sunday Monitor* (Manchester, N.H.), December 19, 1999. Moffitt, *Picturing Extraterrestrials*. Carl Sagan, *The Demon-Haunted World: Science as a Candle in the Dark* (New York: Ballantine, 1997).

6. Michael Shermer, *Why People Believe Weird Things: Pseudoscience, Superstition, and Other Confusions of Our Time* (New York: Freeman, 1997).

7. Gallup and Newport, "Belief in Paranormal Phenomena among Adult Americans. Anonymous, "Poll: U.S. Hiding Knowledge of Aliens," June 15, 1997, CNN Interactive, edition.cnn.com/US/9706/15/ufo.poll (accessed April 2005).

8. Edward Regis Jr., ed., *Extraterrestrials: Science and Alien Intelligence* (Cambridge: Cambridge University Press, 1985).

9. B. A. Maher, "Delusional Thinking and Perceptual Disorder," *Journal of Individual Psychology,* 30 (1974): 98–113. Karl Jaspers, *General Psychopathology* (Chicago: University of Chicago Press, 1963; orig. pub. 1923). Graham F. Reed, *The Psychology of Anomalous Experience: A Cognitive Approach* (Boston: Houghton Mifflin, 1974; orig. pub. 1972). B. A. Maher, "Delusions: Contemporary Etiological Hypotheses," *Psychiatric Annals,* 22 (1992): 260–268.

10. B. A. Maher, "The Irrelevance of Rationality in Adaptive Behavior," in Manfred Spitzer and Brendan A. Maher, eds., *Philosophy and Psychopathology* (New York: Springer-Verlag, 1990), 73–85.

11. Hufford, *The Terror That Comes in the Night.*

3.   Why Do I Have Memories If It Didn't Happen?

1. Robert A. Baker, *Hidden Memories: Voices and Visions from Within* (Buffalo, N.Y.: Prometheus Books, 1992). S. A. Clancy, R. J. McNally, D. L. Schacter, M. F. Lenzenweger, and R. J. Pitman, "Memory Distortion in

People Reporting Abduction by Aliens," *Journal of Abnormal Psychology*, 111, no. 3 (2002): 455–461. Budd Hopkins, *Missing Time* (New York: Berkley, 1983). John E. Mack, *Abduction: Human Encounters with Aliens* (New York: Ballantine, 1995; orig. pub. 1994).

2. John E. Mack, Foreword, in David M. Jacobs, *Secret Life: Firsthand Accounts of UFO Abductions* (New York: Simon and Shuster, 1992), 10.

3. S. J. Lynn, T. Lock, E. F. Loftus, E. Krackow, and S. O. Lilienfeld, "The Remembrance of Things Past: Problematic Memory Recovery Techniques in Psychotherapy," in Scott O. Lilienfeld, Steven Jay Lynn, and Jeffrey M. Lohr, eds., *Science and Pseudoscience in Clinical Psychology* (New York: Guilford Press, 2003), 205–239. M. T. Orne, "The Use and Misuse of Hypnosis in Court," *International Journal of Clinical and Experimental Hypnosis*, 27 (1979): 311–341. Nicholas P. Spanos, *Multiple Identities and False Memories: A Sociocognitive Perspective* (Washington, D.C.: American Psychological Association, 1996).

4. G. K. Ganaway, "Historical versus Narrative Truth: Clarifying the Role of Exogenous Trauma in the Etiology of MPD and Its Variants," *Dissociation*, 2 (1989): 205–220. M. T. Orne, W. G. Whitehouse, D. F. Dinges, and E. C. Orne, "Reconstructing Memory through Hypnosis: Forensic and Clinical Implications," in Helen M. Pettinati, ed., *Hypnosis and Memory* (New York: Guilford Press, 1988), 21–63. N. P. Spanos, E. Menary, N. J. Gabora, S. C. DuBreuil, and B. Dewhirst, "Secondary Identity Enactments during Hypnotic Past-Life Regression: A Sociocognitive Perspective," *Journal of Personality and Social Psychology*, 61 (1991): 308–320.

5. Lynn, Lock, Loftus, Krackow, and Lilienfeld, The Remembrance of Things Past." Mack, *Abduction*. P. Sheehan, "Confidence and Memory in Hypnosis," in Pettinati, ed., Hypnosis and Memory, 95–127. N. M. Steblay and R. K. Bothwell, "Evidence for Hypnotically Refreshed Testimony: The View from the Laboratory," *Law and Human Behavior*, 18 (1994): 635–651. The quotation by John Mack is from Kaja Perina, "Cracking the Harvard X-Files," *Psychology Today* (March–April 2003): 72; online version entitled "Alien Abductions: The Real Deal?" cms .psychologytoday.com/articles/pto-20030527-000002.html (accessed April 2005).

6. J. F. Kihlstrom and I. P. Hoyt, "Hypnosis and the Psychology of Delusions," in Thomas F. Oltmanns and Brendan A. Maher, eds., *Delusional Beliefs: Interdisciplinary Perspectives* (New York: Wiley, 1988).

7. S. J. Lynn, I. Kirsch, A. Barabasz, E. Cardena, and D. Patterson, "Hypnosis as an Empirically Supported Clinical Intervention: The State of

the Evidence and a Look to the Future," *International Journal of Clinical and Experimental Hypnosis,* 48 (2000): 239–259.

8. J. R. Laurence and C. Perry, "Hypnotically Created Memory among Highly Hypnotizable Subjects," *Science,* 222 (1983): 523–524.

9. J. F. Kihlstrom, "Hypnosis," *Annual Review of Psychology,* 36 (1985): 385–418.

10. S. J. Lynn, J. Rhue, and J. P. Weekes, "Hypnotic Involuntariness: A Social-Cognitive Analysis," *Psychological Review,* 97 (1990): 169–184.

11. Robert A. Baker, *Hidden Memories: Voices and Visions from Within* (Buffalo, N.Y.: Prometheus Books, 1992).

12. E. J. Loftus, "The Reality of Repressed Memories," *American Psychologist,* 48 (1993): 518–537.

13. Frederic C. Bartlett, *Remembering: A Study in Experimental and Social Psychology* (Cambridge: Cambridge University Press, 1932). See also R. E. Anderson, "Did I Do It or Did I Only Imagine Doing It?" *Journal of Experimental Psychology: General,* 113 (1984): 594–613. S. A. Clancy, R. J. McNally, and D. L. Schacter, "Effects of Guided Imagery on Memory Distortion in Women Reporting Recovered Memories of Childhood Sexual Abuse," *Journal of Traumatic Stress,* 12 (1999): 559–569. M. Garry, C. G. Manning, E. F. Loftus, and S. J. Sherman, "Imagination Inflation: Imagining a Childhood Event Inflates Confidence That It Occurred," *Psychonomic Bulletin and Review,* 3 (1996): 208–214.

14. M. K. Johnson, "Reality Monitoring: An Experimental Phenomenological Approach," *Journal of Experimental Psychology: General,* 117 (1988): 107–110. M. K. Johnson, S. F. Nolde, and D. M. De Leonardis, "Emotional Focus and Source Monitoring," *Journal of Memory and Language,* 35 (1997): 135–156. M. K. Johnson, S. Hashtroudi, and D. S. Lindsay, "Source Monitoring," *Psychological Bulletin,* 114 (1993): 3–28.

15. M. Garry, C. G. Manning, E. F. Loftus, and S. J. Sherman, "Imagination Inflation: Imagining a Childhood Event Inflates Confidence That It Occurred," *Psychonomic Bulletin and Review,* 3 (1996): 208–214. I. E. Hyman Jr., T. H. Husband, and F. J. Billings, "False Memories of Childhood Experiences," *Applied Cognitive Psychology,* 9 (1995): 181–197.

16. M. K. Johnson, M. A. Foley, A. G. Suengas, and C. L. Raye, "Phenomenal Characteristics of Memories for Perceived and Imagined Autobiographical Events," *Journal of Experimental Psychology: General,* 117 (1988): 371–376.

17. B. Gonsalves, P. J. Reber, D. R. Gitelman, T. B. Parrish, M. M. Mesulam, and K. A. Paller, "Neural Evidence That Vivid Imagining Can Lead to False Remembering," *Psychological Science,* 15 (2004): 655–660.

18. D. L. Schacter, K. A. Norman, and W. Koutstaal, "The Cognitive Neuroscience of Constructive Memory," *Annual Review of Psychology,* 49 (1998): 289–318. Daniel L. Schacter, *Searching for Memory: The Brain, the Mind, and the Past* (New York: Basic Books, 1996).

19. B. A. Maher, "Facts, Irish Facts, Mythofacts, and Interesting Possibilities," in *The View from Room Seventeen: Ten Articles from Brendan A. Maher* (Cambridge, Mass.: Graduate School Alumni Association, Harvard University, 1992), 19–25.

20. Ulric Neisser, *Cognitive Psychology* (New York: Appleton-Century-Crofts, 1967), 285.

21. Schacter, Norman, and Koutstaal, "The Cognitive Neuroscience of Constructive Memory."

22. C. Z. Enns, J. Cambell, C. A. Courtois, M. C. Gottlieb, K. P. Lese, M. S. Gilbert, and L. Forrest, "Working with Adult Clients Who May Have Experienced Childhood Abuse: Recommendations for Assessment and Practice," *Professional Psychology: Research and Practice,* 29 (1998): 245–256. Lynn, Lock, Loftus, Krackow, and Lilienfeld, "The Remembrance of Things Past."

23. M. D. Yapko, "Suggestibility and Repressed Memories of Abuse: A Survey of Psychotherapists' Beliefs," *American Journal of Clinical Hypnosis,* 36 (1994): 163–171.

24. Mack, *Abduction.* David M. Jacobs, *Secret Life: Firsthand Accounts of UFO Abductions* (New York: Simon and Schuster, 1992).

25. Mack, *Abduction,* 144–145, 142.

26. Ibid., 142.

27. R. J. McNally, N. B. Lasko, S. A. Clancy, M. L. Macklin, R. K. Pitman, and S. P. Orr, "Psychophysiologic Responding during Script-Driven Imagery in People Reporting Abduction by Space Aliens," *Psychological Science,* 5 (2004): 493–497.

28. Fyodor Dostoevsky, *Letters of Fyodor Michailovitch Dostoevsky to His Family and Friends,* trans. Ethel Colburn Mayne (New York: Horizon Press, 1961), 289; cited in H. Morgan, "Dostoevsky's Epilepsy: A Case Report and Comparison," *Surgical Neurology,* 33 (1990): 413–416.

4.   Why Are Abduction Stories So Consistent?

1. Keith Thompson, *Angels and Aliens: UFOs and the Mythic Imagination* (New York: Ballantine, 1993). John F. Moffitt, *Picturing Extraterrestrials: Alien Images in Modern Culture* (Amherst, N.Y.: Prometheus Books, 2003). Curtis D. MacDougall, *Superstition and the Press* (Buffalo, N.Y.:

Prometheus Books, 1983), 579. Terry Matheson, *Alien Abductions: Creating a Modern Phenomenon* (Amherst, N.Y.: Prometheus Books, 1998).

2. Albertus Magnus, quoted in Steven J. Dick, *Plurality of Worlds: The Origins of the Extraterrestrial Life Debate from Democritus to Kant* (Cambridge: Cambridge University Press, 1983), 23, trans. Steven J. Dick.

3. Epicurus, "Letter to Herodotus," trans. C. Bailey, in Whitney J. Oates, ed., *The Stoic and Epicurean Philosophers* (New York: Modern Library, 1957), 3–15.

4. Michael J. Crowe, *The Extraterrestrial Life Debate, 1750–1990* (Mineola, N.Y.: Dover, 1999).

5. Johann Bode, cited ibid., 73.

6. Physicist Lee Smolin, cited in Stephen Webb, *If the Universe Is Teeming with Aliens . . . Where Is Everybody? Fifty Solutions to the Fermi Paradox and the Problem of Extraterrestrial Life* (New York: Copernicus Books, 2002), 24.

7. I. S. Shklovskii and Carl Sagan, eds., *Intelligent Life in the Universe* (New York: Bantam, 1966), 357.

8. Pseudo-Plutarch, *Placita Philosophorum,* ch. 30, cited in G. McColley, "The Seventeenth-Century Doctrine of a Plurality of Worlds," *Annals of Science,* 1 (1936): 386–387.

9. Nicholas of Cusa, *Of Learned Ignorance,* trans. Germain Heron (London: Routledge and Kegan Paul, 1954), 114–115.

10. Bernard Le Bovier, sieur de Fontenelle, *Entretiens sur la pluralité des mondes* (1686), in English as *A Plurality of Worlds,* trans. John Glanvill (London: R. Bentley and S. Magnes, 1688), cited in L. M. Marfak, ed., *The Achievement of Bernard Le Bovier de Fontenelle* (New York: Johnson Reprints, 1970), 96, 121.

11. C. K. Hofling, "Percival Lowell and the Canals of Mars," *British Journal of Medical Psychology,* 37 (1964): 33–42.

12. Carl Sagan, quoted in F. J. Tipler, "Additional Remarks on Extraterrestrial Intelligence," *Royal Astronomical Society Quarterly Journal,* 22 (1981): 279–292.

13. Immanuel Kant, quoted in Crowe, *The Extraterrestrial Life Debate,* 97.

14. Emanuel Swedenborg, *Heaven and Hell,* ed. G. F. Dole (New York: Swedenborg Foundation, 1984). Emanuel Swedenborg, *Arcana Coelestia,* vol. 1, in English as *Concerning the Earths in Our Solar System, Which Are Called Planets, and Concerning the Earths in the Starry Heavens* (Boston: O. Clapp, 1839).

15. "Golden-Haired Girl Is In It: The Airship Discovered . . .," *St. Louis Post-Dispatch* (April 19, 1897), 1.

16. Anonymous, "That Airship: Farmer Near Josserand Conversed with the Crew," *Houston Post* (April 26, 1897), 2.

17. Hadley Cantril, *The Invasion from Mars: A Study of the Psychology of Panic* (Princeton, N.J.: Princeton University Press, 1982; orig. pub. 1940). The latest incarnation of Wells's story is Steven Spielberg's film *War of the Worlds* (Paramount Pictures, 2005).

18. Desmond Leslie and George Adamski, *Flying Saucers Have Landed* (London: W. Laurie, 1953).

19. Carl Sagan, *The Demon-Haunted World: Science as a Candle in the Dark* (New York: Ballantine, 1997), 101.

20. David J. Schow and Jeffrey Frentzen, *The Outer Limits: The Official Companion* (New York: Ace Science Fiction Books, 1986).

21. For a review, see Robert E. Bartholomew and George S. Howard, *UFOs and Alien Contact: Two Centuries of Mystery* (Amherst, N.Y.: Prometheus Books, 1998).

22. For these and other citations drawn from the initial media reportage, see Keith Thompson, *Angels and Aliens: UFOs and the Mythic Imagination* (New York: Ballantine, 1993), 1–5.

23. Associated Press dispatch, quoted in Curtis D. MacDougall, *Superstition and the Press* (Buffalo, N.Y.: Prometheus Books, 1983), 579.

24. For these reports, see Kendrick Frazier, Barry Karr, and Joe Nickell, eds., *The UFO Invasion: The Roswell Incident, Alien Abductions, and Government Coverups* (Amherst, N.Y.: Prometheus Books, 1997), 96, 125.

25. John F. Moffitt, *Picturing Extraterrestrials: Alien Images in Modern Culture* (Amherst, N.Y.: Prometheus Books, 2003).

26. Charles Berlitz and William L. Moore, *The Roswell Incident* (New York: Grosset and Dunlap, 1980), 296.

27. Kal K. Korff, "What Really Happened at Roswell," *Skeptical Inquirer* (July–August 1997): 24–31. Philip J. Klass, *The Real Roswell Crashed-Saucer Coverup* (Amherst, N.Y.: Prometheus Books, 1997). Kal K. Korff, *The Roswell UFO Crash: What They Don't Want You To Know* (New York: Dell, 2000).

28. Donald Keyhoe, *The Flying Saucers Are Real* (New York: Fawcett, 1950).

29. Frank Scully, *Behind the Flying Saucers* (New York: Popular Library, 1951).

30. Gerald Heard, *The Riddle of the Flying Saucers: Is Another World Watching?* (London: Carroll and Nicholson, 1950). The book was published in the United States under the main title *Is Another World Watching?* (New York: Harper, 1951).

31. On the Betty and Barney Hill story, see the following: J. Nickell, "Ex-

traterrestrial Iconography," *Skeptical Inquirer,* 21 (1997): 19. Matheson, *Alien Abductions.* Philip J. Klass, *UFO Abductions: A Dangerous Game* (Buffalo, N.Y.: Prometheus Books, 1988). Thompson, *Angels and Aliens.* Moffitt, *Picturing Extraterrestrials.*

32. All excerpts from the Hills, transcripts are taken from John Grant Fuller, *The Interrupted Journey: Two Lost Hours "Aboard a Flying Saucer"* (New York: Dial, 1966). Fuller inexplicably chose to publish the complete transcripts of the hypnosis sessions along with his own account, which varied significantly from the transcripts.

33. Klass, *UFO Abductions,* 42.

34. Travis Walton, *The Walton Experience* (New York: Berkley, 1978).

35. Raymond E. Fowler, *The Andreasson Affair* (New York: Bantam, 1980; orig. pub. 1979), 88.

36. All quotes ibid., 27–29, 41–43.

37. John E. Mack, *Abduction: Human Encounters with Aliens* (New York: Ballantine, 1995; orig. pub. 1994).

38. All quotes from Whitley Strieber, *Communion: A True Story* (New York: Avon, 1987), 60, 61, 94.

39. A. H. Lawson and W. C. McCall, "Hypnosis of Imaginary UFO Abductees," paper presented at the meeting of the American Psychological Association, Toronto, 1978.

40. T. E. Bullard, "UFO Abduction Reports: The Supernatural Kidnap Narrative Returns in Technological Guise," *Journal of American Folklore,* 102 (1989): 147–170. John Rimmer, *The Evidence for Alien Abductions* (Wellingborough, U.K.: Aquarian, 1984).

41. Mack, *Abduction,* 11.

42. Online at http://entertainment.news.designerz.com/close-encounters-on-rise-as-ufos-seize-imagination-of-chinese.html.

43. Carl Jung, *Flying Saucers: A Modern Myth of Things Seen in the Sky* (Princeton, N.J.: Princeton University Press, 1973), 13–14.

5. Who Gets Abducted?

1. S. A. Clancy, R. J. McNally, D. L. Schacter, M. F. Lenzenweger, and R. J. Pitman, "Memory Distortion in People Reporting Abduction by Aliens," *Journal of Abnormal Psychology,* 111, no. 3 (2002): 455–461. C. C. McLeod, M. L. O'Connell, R. L. Colasanti, J. E. Mack, "Anomalous Experience and Psychopathology: The Questions of Alien Abduction," unpublished manuscript. N. P. Spanos, P. A. Cross, I. Dickson, and S. C. DuBreuil "Close Encounters: An Examination of UFO Experiences," *Journal of Abnormal Psychology,* 102 (1993): 624–632.

2. M. F. Lenzenweger and L. Korfine, "Identifying Schizophrenia-Related Personality Disorder Features in a Nonclinical Population Using a Psychometric Approach," *Journal of Personality Disorders,* 6 (1992): 256–266. M. F. Lenzenweger, "Deeper into the Schizotypy Taxon: On the Robust Nature of Maximum Covariance Analysis," *Journal of Abnormal Psychology,* 108 (1999): 182–187. P. E. Meehl, "Schizotaxia, Schizotypy, Schizophrenia," *American Psychologist,* 17 (1962): 827–838.

3. Clancy, McNally, Schacter, Lenzenweger, and Pitman, "Memory Distortion in People Reporting Abduction by Aliens," 455–461. J. Chequers, S. Joseph, and D. Diduca, "Belief in Extraterrestrial Life, UFO-Related Beliefs, and Schizotypal Personality," *Personality and Individual Differences,* 23 (1997): 519–521.

4. J. Maltby and L. Day, "Religious Experience, Religious Orientation and Schizotypy," *Mental Health, Religion and Culture,* 5 (2002): 163–174. D. Watson, "Dissociations of the Night: Individual Differences in Sleep-Related Experiences and Their Relation to Dissociation and Schizotypy," *Journal of Abnormal Psychology,* 110 (2001): 426–535.

5. M. Wilson, "DSM-III and the Transformation of American Psychiatry: A History," *American Journal of Psychiatry,* 150 (1993): 399–410.

6. Elaine Showalter, *Hystories: Hysterical Epidemics and Modern Media* (New York: Columbia University Press, 1997).

7. S. M. Powers, "Dissociation in Alleged Extraterrestrial Abductees," *Dissociation: Progress in the Dissociative Disorders,* 7 (1994): 44–50. J. Takhar and S. Fisman, "Alien Abduction in PTSD," *Journal of the American Academy of Child and Adolescent Psychiatry,* 34 (1995): 974–975.

8. R. Porter, "The Body and the Mind, the Doctor and the Patient: Negotiating Hysteria," in Sander Gilman, Helen King, Roy Porter, G. S. Rousseau, and Elaine Showalter, *Hysteria beyond Freud* (Berkeley: University of California Press, 1993), 235.

9. A. N. Chowdhury, "A Hundred Years of Koro: The History of a Culture-Bound Syndrome," *International Journal of Social Psychiatry,* 44 (1998): 181–188.

10. See S. C. Wilson and T. X. Barber, "The Fantasy-Prone Personality: Implications for Understanding Imagery, Hypnosis, and Parapsychological Phenomena," in Anees A. Sheikh, ed., *Imagery: Current Theory, Research, and Application* (New York: Wiley, 1983), 340–390. Sheryl Wilson and Theodore Barber were the first to describe the fantasy-prone personality.

11. R. E. Bartholomew, K. Basterfield, and G. S. Howard, "UFO Abductees and Contactees: Psychopathology or Fantasy-Proneness?" *Professional Psychology: Research and Practice,* 22 (1991): 215–222. P. Bowers, "Hyp-

notizability, Creativity, and the Role of Effortless Experiencing," *International Journal of Clinical and Experimental Hypnosis*, 26 (1978): 184–202. H. J. Irwin, "Fantasy Proneness and Paranormal Beliefs," *Psychological Reports*, 66 (1990): 655–658. S. J. Lynn and I. I. Kirsch, "Alleged Alien Abductions: False Memories, Hypnosis, and Fantasy Proneness," *Psychological Inquiry*, 7, no. 2 (1996): 151–155. S. J. Lynn and J. W. Rhue, "Fantasy Proneness: Hypnosis, Developmental Antecedents, and Psychopathology," *American Psychologist*, 43 (1988): 35–44. L. S. Milling, I. Kirsch, and C. Burgess, "Hypnotic Suggestibility and Absorption: Revisiting the Context Effect," *Contemporary Hypnosis*, 17 (2000): 32–41. S. M. Roche and K. M. McConkey, "Absorption: Nature, Assessment, and Correlates," *Journal of Personality and Social Psychology*, 59 (1990): 91–101. A. Tellegan and G. Atkinson, "Openness to Absorbing and Self-Altering Experiences ('Absorption'), a Trait Related to Hypnotic Susceptibility," *Journal of Abnormal Psychology*, 83 (1974): 268–277. S. C. Wilson, and T. X. Barber, "The Creative Imagination Scale as a Measure of Hypnotic Responsiveness: Application to Experimental and Clinical Hypnosis," *American Journal of Clinical Hypnosis*, 20 (1978): 235–249.

12. Bartholomew, Basterfield, and Howard, "UFO Abductees and Contactees." Robert E. Bartholomew and George S. Howard, *UFOs and Alien Contact: Two Centuries of Mystery* (Amherst, N.Y.: Prometheus Books, 1998). Clancy, McNally, Schacter, Lenzenweger, and Pitman, "Memory Distortion in People Reporting Abduction by Aliens."

13. False-memory syndrome was clinically defined by John F. Kihlstrom (though he was not the first to use the term). See Kihlstrom, "Exhumed Memory," in Steven Jay Lynn and Kevin M. McConkey, eds., *Truth in Memory* (New York: Guilford Press, 1998).

14. J. Deese, "On the Prediction of Occurrence of Particular Verbal Intrusions in Immediate Recall," *Journal of Experimental Psychology*, 58 (1959): 17–22. K. J. Robinson and H. L. Roediger III, "Associative Processes in False Recall and False Recognition," *Psychological Science*, 8 (1997): 231–237. H. L. Roediger III and K. B. McDermott, "Creating False Memories? Remembering Words Not Presented in Lists," *Journal of Experimental Psychology: Learning, Memory, and Cognition*, 21 (1995): 803–814.

15. Clancy, McNally, Schacter, Lenzenweger, and Pitman, "Memory Distortion in People Reporting Abduction by Aliens."

16. N. P. Spanos, E. Menary, N. J. Gabora, S. C. DuBreuil, and B. Dewhirst, "Secondary Identity Enactments during Hypnotic Past-Life Regres-

sion: A Sociocognitive Perspective," *Journal of Personality and Social Psychology*, 61 (1991): 308–320. N. P. Spanos, C. A. Burgess, and M. F. Burgess, "Past-Life Identities, UFO Abductions and Satanic Ritual Abuse: The Social Construction of 'Memories,'" *International Journal of Clinical and Experimental Hypnosis*, 42 (1994): 433–446.

6.   If It Didn't Happen, Why Would I Want To Believe It Did?

1. National Academy of Sciences, "Review of the University of Colorado Report on Unidentified Flying Objects by a Panel of the National Academy of Sciences" (1969), 6. Online at www.project1947.com/shg/articles/nascu.html (accessed April 2005).

2. P. A. Sturrock et al., "Physical Evidence of UFO Reports: The Proceedings of a Workshop Held at the Pocantico Conference Center, Tarrytown, New York, September 29–October 4, 1997," *Journal of Scientific Exploration*, 12 (1998): 179–229.

3. Stephen Webb, *If the Universe Is Teeming with Aliens . . . Where Is Everybody? Fifty Solutions to the Fermi Paradox and the Problem of Extraterrestrial Life* (New York: Copernicus Books, 2002).

4. L. S. Newman and R. F. Baumeister, "Toward an Elaboration of the UFO Abduction Phenomenon: Hypnotic Elaboration, Extraterrestrial Sadomasochism, and Spurious Memories," *Psychological Inquiry*, 7, no. 2 (1996): 99–126. S. J. Lynn and I. I. Kirsch, "Alleged Alien Abductions: False Memories, Hypnosis, and Fantasy-Proneness," *Psychological Inquiry*, 7, no. 2 (1966): 151–155. M. R. Banaji and J. F. Kihlstrom, "The Ordinary Nature of Alien-Abduction Memories," *Psychological Inquiry*, 7, no. 2 (1996): 132–135.

5. R. J. McNally and S. A. Clancy, "Sleep Paralysis, Sexual Abuse, and Space Alien Abduction," *Transcultural Psychiatry*, 42 (2005): 113–122. S. E. Clark and E. F. Loftus, "The Construction of Space Alien Memories," *Psychological Inquiry*, 7 (1996): 140–143. R. E. Bartholomew, K. Basterfield, and G. S. Howard, "UFO Abductees and Contactees: Psychopathology or Fantasy-Proneness?" *Professional Psychology: Research and Practice*, 22 (1991): 215–222. Robert E. Bartholomew and George S. Howard, *UFOs and Alien Contact: Two Centuries of Mystery* (Amherst, N.Y.: Prometheus Books, 1998).

6. David M. Jacobs, *Secret Life: Firsthand Accounts of UFO Abductions* (New York: Simon and Shuster, 1992), 26. John E. Mack, Foreword, in Jacobs, *Secret Life*, 9.

7. Newman and Baumeister, "Toward an Elaboration of the UFO Abduc-

tion Phenomenon," 100. See also L. S. Newman and R. F. Baumeister, "Abducted by Aliens: Spurious Memories of Interplanetary Masochism," in Steven Jay Lynn and Kevin M. McConkey, eds., *Truth in Memory* (New York: Guilford Press, 1998), 284–303.

8. Philip Klass, quoted in Stephan Rae, "John Mack," *New York Times Magazine*, March 20, 1994.

9. Richard Ofshe and Ethan Watters, *Making Monsters: False Memories, Psychotherapy and Sexual Hysteria* (New York: Scribner's, 1994).

10. Frederic C. Bartlett, *Remembering: A Study in Experimental and Social Psychology* (Cambridge: Cambridge University Press, 1932).

11. Frederick Crews, *The Memory Wars: Freud's Legacy in Dispute* (New York: New York Review of Books, 1995).

12. K. Bowers and P. Farvolden, "Revisiting a Century-Old Freudian Slip: From Suggestion Disavowed to Truth Repressed," *Psychological Bulletin*, 119, no. 3 (1996): 355–380.

13. Donald P. Spence, *Narrative Truth and Historical Truth: Meaning and Interpretation in Psychoanalysis* (New York: Norton, 1982), 25.

14. Keith Thomas, *Religion and the Decline of Magic: Studies in Popular Beliefs in Sixteenth and Seventeenth Century England* (London: Weidenfeld and Nicolson, 1971), esp. 21.

15. Nicholas P. Spanos, *Multiple Identities and False Memories: A Sociocognitive Perspective* (Washington, D.C.: American Psychological Association, 1996).

16. C. H. Thigpen and H. Cleckley, "On the Incidence of Multiple Personality Disorder: A Brief Communication," *International Journal of Clinical and Experimental Hypnosis,* 32 (1984): 63–66.

17. R. J. McNally, N. B. Lasko, S. A. Clancy, M. L. Macklin, R. K. Pitman, and S. P. Orr, "Psychophysiological Responding during Script-Driven Imagery in People Reporting Abduction by Space Aliens," *Psychological Science,* 15 (2004): 493–497.

18. Carl Sagan, *The Demon-Haunted World: Science as a Candle in the Dark* (New York: Ballantine, 1997), 15.

19. Ibid., 187.

20. R. F. Baumeister and L. S. Newman, "How Stories Make Sense of Personal Experiences: Motives That Shape Autobiographical Narratives," *Personality and Social Psychology Bulletin,* 20 (1994): 676–690. M. H. Erdelyi, "Repression: The Mechanism and the Defense," in Daniel M. Wegner and James W. Pennebaker, eds., *Handbook of Mental Control* (Englewood Cliffs, N.J.: Prentice Hall, 1993), 126–148. M. Ross, "Rela-

tion of Implicit Theories to the Construction of Personal Histories," *Psychological Review,* 96 (1989): 341–357.

21. This sculpture, also known as *The Ecstasy of Saint Theresa,* was completed in 1652 and is now in the Church of Santa Maria della Vittoria, Rome.

22. Theresa of Avila, *Libro de la vida.* In English, *The Life of Saint Teresa,* trans. and ed. J. M. Cohen (Harmondsworth: Penguin, 1957), 209–211.

23. Raymond E. Fowler, *The Andreasson Affair* (New York: Bantam, 1980; orig. pub. 1979), 50–51.

24. Budd Hopkins, in "Alien Abduction Claims and Standards of Inquiry," Transcript from radio program *Extension 720,* hosted by M. Rosenberg, WGN Radio, Chicago, *Skeptical Inquirer,* 12 (1988): 270–278.

25. Carl Jung, *Flying Saucers: A Modern Myth of Things Seen in the Sky* (Princeton, N.J.: Princeton University Press, 1973).

26. Bertolt Brecht, *Leben des Galilei* (1940). In English, *Galileo,* trans. Charles Laughton, ed. Eric Bentley (New York: Grove Press, 1966), scene 7.

Index

Schacter, Daniel, 14
Schizophrenia, 45, 129–130
Schizotypy, 129–130, 134
Science: evidence in, 3–4, 7–8, 27, 28, 41–
45, 77–78, 149–151; Mack on, 4, 5, 7;
ignorance of, 6, 138, 149–150; Sagan
on, 9–10, 149–150; vs. pseudoscience,
10, 149–151; peer review process in,
17; as pursuit of truth, 19, 28; principle of parsimony in, 27, 28, 44, 45, 52,
159n8; impartiality in, 148
Scully, Frank: Behind the Flying Saucers, 94
Search for Extraterrestrial Intelligence
(SETI) Institute, 41, 118, 160n4
Self-help books, 145
Sexual abuse in childhood: repressed
memories of, 11–14, 15–19, 21, 29, 32,
39, 40, 132; and therapists, 12, 13, 14,
16, 30; and multiple personality disorder, 14; vs. alien abduction, 20, 77,
140–142, 144
Sexuality: of aliens, 1, 2, 8, 24, 26, 82,
101, 103, 104, 105, 107, 114, 152; hybrid children, 1, 2, 8, 114, 142, 152;
sexual dysfunction, 38, 47, 57, 101,
142, 149
Shawna (abductee), 34
Shermer, Michael, 7
Shostak, Seth, 41
Simon, Benjamin, 94–95
Sleep paralysis: attitudes of abductees to-
ward, 7, 8, 27, 34–35, 38–39, 48–50,
54–55, 57, 68, 71, 78, 118; definition
and incidence, 35–36; McNally on, 138
Smolin, Lee, 84–85
Somatization disorder, 131
Source-monitoring errors. See Reality-
monitoring errors
Spanos, Nicholas, 144
Spence, Donald: Narrative Truth and His-
torical Truth, 142–143
Spielberg, Steven: Close Encounters of the
Third Kind, 38, 39, 97, 101, 102, 118,
126
Spirit possession, 131
Spiritual healing, 3
Steve (abductee), 118–119

Steven (abductee), 109
Strieber, Whitley, 3; Communion, 39, 58,
66, 100–101, 111–112, 117, 119, 126,
128
Swedenborg, Emanuel: Arcana coelestia,
87

Taoism, 120
Tarot cards, 134
Telepathy, 129
Television programs, 24, 55, 58, 59, 71,
82, 83; X-Files, 7, 66, 103; Mork and
Mindy, 38; Roswell, 38; Third Rock from
the Sun, 38; CSI: Crime Scene Investiga-
tion, 42, 72; The Outer Limits, 89, 95, 97;
alien abductions in, 89, 95, 97, 98–99,
102, 128; South Park, 103–104
Terry (abductee), 33, 75, 76
Therapists: and recovered memories of
sexual abuse, 12, 13, 14, 16, 30; role in
creation of false memories, 12, 13, 14,
16, 25, 26, 40, 57–64, 67, 68, 71–77,
78, 94–99, 101, 117, 119, 135, 136, 138
Theresa of Avila, St., 152–153, 171n21
Thigpen, Corbett, 144
Thomas, Keith, 144
Three Faces of Eve, The (book), 144
Three Faces of Eve, The (motion picture),
59
Time lapses, 38, 117, 127
Tom (abductee), 111–112

Unconscious, the: projection, 104; and
hysteria, 130–131
Unidentified flying objects (UFOs), 83,
91–99, 110; Mutual UFO Network,
Inc. (MUFON), 4, 25, 73; media references to, 25, 37, 93–94; attitudes of
abductees toward, 27, 42–43, 82, 101,
102, 109, 115–117, 118, 119, 120, 124–
125, 127, 152; flying saucers, 89, 91–
94, 95, 104, 116–117; Roswell incident,
92–94, 116; National Academy of Sciences on, 137
U.S. government, 3, 94